PEOPLE *and* COMPETENCIES

PEOPLE *and* COMPETENCIES

COMPETENCIES

The Route to Competitive Advantage

SECOND EDITION

Edited by
**Nick Boulter, Murray Dalziel
and Jackie Hill**
Foreword by
David McClelland

Hay/McBer

KOGAN
PAGE

First published in French as *Des Compétences et des Hommes* in 1992 by Les Editions d'Organisation, Paris

Published in 1992 by Kogan Page Ltd as *Competency Based Human Resource Management*

Reprinted 1992, 1993 (twice)
This edition published in 1996
Reprinted 1997

Kogan Page Limited
120 Pentonville Road
London N1 9JN

British Library Cataloguing in Publication Data

A CIP record for this book is available from the British Library

ISBN 0 7494 2118 5

Typeset by Saxon Graphics Ltd, Derby
Printed and bound in Great Britain by
Biddles Ltd, Guildford and King's Lynn

Contents

Contents

List of Contributors

Heather Bell is a Director of the Hay Group and has been involved in a wide range of assignments using competencies to improve managerial capability, support organisational change, add clarity to roles and increase recruitment effectiveness. During her six years at Hay, Heather's main engagements have been with such clients as Bank of Ireland, Lloyds, Safeway, Sainsbury, PepsiCo and National Grid. Prior to joining Hay, Heather worked for ICI in sales and marketing including a number of management roles.

Daniel Bouchard is a Senior Consultant at Hay specialising in Human Resources Professional Development (HRPD). Daniel has worked extensively with the design and application of competency models and the design and implementation of performance management systems. Working with a major bank, Daniel was involved in defining a competency model for directors and enhancing the assessment process. As part of a project for Banque Neuflize-Schlumberger Mallet, he took part in designing and implementing a competency-based HR development process in a period of business and culture change. A project for Case Europe included designing a competency-based selection process for the re-organised marketing and sales functions in France, Germany and the UK. Before joining Hay, Daniel was a line manager in various commercial and human resources functions.

Nick Boulter is a Senior Director at Hay, where he has been a consultant for 14 years. Nick has helped a range of international companies introduce more effective ways for selecting and developing senior managers with outstanding potential. He consults on competency-based applications for performance and reward management. He also has accountability for Hay's Information Business in Europe.

Dr James Burruss is a Vice President at McBer & Company. His expertise in organisational leadership and human resources management reflects more than 20 years of experience with private and public sector organisations around the world. As a principal and senior officer at McBer, Dr Burruss was responsible for the quality and delivery of most of McBer's products and services and for the management and development of the key consulting staff. His consulting and training experience has primarily focused on mid- and senior-level managers and entrepreneurs. Dr Burruss has taught the human motivation course at Harvard College and was instrumental in developing a highly successful programme for improving the academic performance of minority students at Harvard.

Murray Dalziel is currently General Manager of the Hay Group in Europe. He is also a professional leader in management and organisational development. He has led succession planing and leadership profile assignments in companies such as ICI, BOC and British Petroleum. Over the years he has consulted with PepsiCo, Unilever, Mars, National Power, US Army, 20th Century Fox, Rohm Haas and General Electric. Prior to Hay in Europe, he was with McBer in Boston, Mass. for nine years. He holds a PhD in Sociology from Harvard University and an MA from the University of Edinburgh. He is the co-author of *Changing Ways* with Steven Schooner and *Competency Based Human Resources Management* with David Fitt and Alain Mitrani which won Book of the Year for European Management.

Chris Dyson is a Senior Director of the Hay Group and leads the UK Hay/McBer practice. After 20 years in senior positions with blue chip companies, Chris' ten years in consulting have been focused on raising organisational performance, helping clients achieve step changes in results.

Dr Mary Fontaine is a Senior Vice President and General Manager of the Hay/McBer Innovation and Resource Centre. Since 1980, she has worked with global corporations including PepsiCo, Mobil Oil and IBM, to enhance their leadership capability through competency-based executive recruitment, selection, assessment and development. She has personally assessed and coached hundreds of executives during that time. Dr Fontaine earned her BSc, Phi Beta Kappa and PhD at the University of North Carolina at Chapel Hill where she concentrated in Organisational Behaviour. She also served on the faculty and taught MBA and executive leadership courses for several years at Duke University's Fuqua School of Business.

Frank Hartle is a Director at Hay and the leader of Hay's UK Performance Management Practice. He has been closely involved in a number of major performance management competency assignments in banking, utility and chemicals organisations along with government and local authority work. Prior to joining Hay in 1985, Frank worked in the local education service and was a member of the Executive Committee of the Society of Education Officers. He has written a Performance Management Guide for Head Teachers and has contributed to Hay's book *Competency Based Human Resources Management*. His new book, *How to Re-engineer the Performance Management Process* has recently been published by Kogan Page.

Jackie Hill has been a consultant in Hay since the beginning of 1996 and has been involved in a range of projects using competencies including job family modelling, role profiling, and focused interview training. She has also been involved in a project to review the use of competencies in a large international company. Prior to Hay, Jackie worked in the IT industry in customer and line management and during that time led a project to re-organise a software development company from a functional, hierarchical structure to a matrix organisation. Other deliverables from the project included the definition of new jobs in the product development area and a company-wide job measurement and career structure framework.

Erin Lap has ten year's experience with the Hay Group working with a wide variety of organisations. Erin is the Human Resources Professional Development Practice Leader in the Netherlands.

John Larrere is Senior Vice President of McBer & Company. His areas of expertise include competency research, the professional development of internal consultants, the design and implementation of management development programmes and organisational improvement interventions. He is also the architect of McBer's managerial coaching technology. John directs Hay/McBer's Human Resources Planning and Development Practice in Latin America and also works extensively in Europe. John has researched competency models in a variety of contexts, enabling his clients to determine what enables outstanding performance in particular jobs. He has conducted research into leadership as exercised in business, the military, sales, education, health care and religious institutions. He has assisted his clients in applying the results of his research to selection, selection interviewing, professional development and career pathing. The organisational improvement initiatives that John has planned and delivered focus on increased organisational performance in the areas of efficiency, quality and customer service.

Patricia Marshall is Technical Development Director for Hay/McBer Europe. Her consulting is in human resource management, particularly in competency based selection, assessment and career development. The clients she works with include Sun Life Assurance, Unilever, Texaco, Health Authorities, Bank of Ireland, Volvo Car Corporation and PepsiCo. Patricia received her BA in Psychology and French from the National University of Ireland and her MSc in Occupational Psychology from the University of Hertford. She is a Chartered Occupational Psychologist and an Associate Fellow of the British Psychological Society. She is also a member of the BPS's Special Group in Counselling Psychology.

Axel Peters is a Human Resources specialist with experience in management development, training and training media, organisational development, compensation and benefits. Much of his career has been spent as an internal or external consultant with experience prior to Hay in Nixdorf Computer AG. He has also worked as a line manager at Innomedia, a joint venture between Nixdorf and Bertelsmann. At Hay, Axel has worked on several major projects for

List of contributors

Citibank, Commerzbank, Kreditanstalt Fur Wiederaufbau, Mazda Motors, Quelle, Treuhandanstalt, giving advice on organisation, compensation and benefits and performance appraisal.

Derek Pritchard is a Director of Hay, specialising in job measurement and job evaluation in the UK and Europe. He began his career as a research scientist in industry before becoming General Manager of a group in the plastics industry. He has contributed articles on job evaluation, pay and incentives to a number of journals and magazines.

Sylvia De Voge is head of the Organisational Change Practice for Hay in the UK. She has extensive experience in designing and implementing organisational change in complex organisations, both in the US and the UK. She specialises in working with companies to realise strategy through people and has worked with large plcs in the finance, manufacturing and FMCG sectors, helping them to design and manage major organisational change. She also has extensive experience in helping companies to make the major shift required for privatisation. Sylvia has a BA (Distinction) from Texas A & M University. In addition to her full-time commitment to Hay, Sylvia is the Visiting Lecturer for Corporate Strategy and Strategy Implementation for the part-time MBA programme at Durham University.

David C McClelland is the founder and chairman of the board of McBer & Company. A former professor of psychology at Harvard University, Dr McClelland has devoted a lifetime to research that has resulted in an internationally accepted theory of human motivation. His theory and research findings have been applied to management, small-business administration, post-secondary education, mental health, behavioural medicine, economic development and the modernisation of developing countries.

Author of *The Achieving Society* and *Power: The Inner Experience*, Dr McClelland is widely published on human motivation and related topics.

Dr McClelland received his BA in Psychology and Sociology from Wesleyan University; his MA in Psychology from the

University of Missouri; and his PhD in Psychology from Yale University. He holds honorary doctorates in science, philosophy, law and literature.

Foreword

Dr David McClelland

At the inauguration of the McClelland Institute in Singapore a few years ago, it occurred to me to begin at the beginning — to begin by trying to define what a business is, since we are in the business of trying to help businesses do better. So just what is a business and what is it trying to do? I came up with the following definition:

> A good business is a community of individuals organised to provide worthwhile (useful or needed) goods or services in a way which brings maximum long-term satisfaction to its participants, or as they are sometimes called, its stakeholders — its owners, producers and customers.

Such a definition is very broad and covers just about every conceivable kind of business, including non-profit making organisations where satisfaction to owners or customers may be measured in non-monetary terms. It also inevitably leads to discussions of what is 'worthwhile'. Some will want to argue that selling alcohol or cigarettes are not worthwhile services, but what is important here is not that we settle such issues, but that we accept as a goal that business should provide useful goods and services and that a business involves collaboration among many individuals whose goal is to maximise satisfaction of all participants in the community of interest.

My audience was pleased with my definition — which is part of the reason I repeat it here. I think it made business sound really

respectable and worthwhile in the same sense that people generally regard social work of helping people in need as worthwhile.
Business has often received a bad rap — because there are of course
bad businessmen who exploit their workers or cheat their customers — but that should not detract from understanding that our
calling is fundamentally to service. This may seem hopelessly naive
and old-fashioned yet I have never forgotten the genuine zeal with
which my Quaker father-in-law sold blow-off valves and steam
traps for steam systems. He really thought of himself as providing
important products and services because he remembered what it
was like not to have safe and clean steam transmission lines which
would interfere with customer satisfaction and cost consumers
money. As a minister's son, it quite frankly had never occurred to
me that helping 10, 000 people to have more reliably heated homes
was as worthwhile as feeding a hungry child. But as I have grown
up I have been a little puzzled that relief work to feed hungry
Indian children can lead to elevation to sainthood but not the
invention of a new kind of rice which keeps thousands of Indian
children from starving to death.

But be that as it may, it has become part of my mission to encourage business people into thinking they can do wonderfully worthwhile things. It is my conviction that fast food companies like
McDonald's have done more to help the hungry than many soup
kitchens. McDonald's provides the means by collecting empties to
purchase food very inexpensively that can provide a good diet and
it is not a demeaning handout. Yet when do they get credit for providing services to the poor?

The definition also calls attention to the fact that business provides
not only a worthwhile service but is a very collaborative enterprise.
People have to work together to produce goods and services and to
maximise everyone's satisfaction. Traditionally that realisation has
led business experts to try and design systems which will facilitate
working together by dividing up the work and parcelling out
responsibility for decision-making and leadership of various groups.

Yet over the past century we have slowly begun to realise that
there are real limitations to just trying to redesign work so that people can work together more easily and productively. Recently I was
called in to take part in a discussion about how to facilitate the func-

tioning of teams. As would be expected, attention was first turned to such matters as being sure there is a clear sense of mission for the team, a proper assignment of tasks to different members of the team, good informational and organisation supports for the team, proper resources to work with, etc. All of these things are clearly needed — without them the team couldn't function — yet I kept feeling that you could have all these things like a well-designed Swiss watch — but the team might still not go. Why? Because fundamentally it is people with certain competencies that make teams go.

It reminds me of a simple illustration of the principle taken from former times when families often got together at Thanksgiving to prepare and enjoy a feast. There were usually several people in the kitchen — the team — whose clear goal was to get the food on the table at a reasonable hour. People were usually assigned various tasks. There were ample supplies and a good information system as they chattered with each other about what they were doing. The food always did get on the table in good order for a happy meal but I was often astonished at the reactions afterwards of some of those who had been in the kitchen. They would say things like: 'Cathy was wonderful; she was always there when needed, she knew what to do without being asked, it was a joy to have her helping.' Or, 'S was such a problem; she never seemed to know what to do; she kept asking, "what shall I do now?", and making me interrupt what I was doing to try to help her out.' One suspects that no amount of careful role assignment would have cleared up S's problem. She just didn't have the organisational awareness of what was going on and the interpersonal sensitivity to know who was in need of help at which point — both being competencies that we have found facilitate teamwork.

So design of work is important but the best design in the world for how a team should work will be dead at the start without some people like Cathy. People with team oriented competencies build the teams' priorities and work habits as they get practice with each other. They must learn to be flexible and respond effectively in terms of novel situations that the preplanners could not have anticipated. That is why building on competencies enhances competitive advantage.

But how many Cathys are there in the world? How do we locate them? Suppose we agree they are needed. Aren't they hard to find and expensive to hire because they are scarce? The question reminds me of a conversation I had many years ago with a North American businessman who had made quite a success in Mexico. He knew I was there in an effort to train Mexican businessmen to have more Achievement motivation which he readily agreed with me was a key part of entrepreneurial success.

But he insisted I was wasting my time trying to train Mexicans to take moderate risks, plan ahead more carefully for the best way of accomplishing something, etc. It just wasn't in their nature he said. Mexican business would have to rely on outsiders like himself who had a real feel for business. Well, history has clearly proved him wrong, as the current young excellent group of Mexican business-men proves. But the doubt is still with us: Where are we going to get the people with all the competencies we need, not only for teamwork, but for all sorts of new business challenges in new parts of the world?

The good news is that competencies can be taught and learned. We showed conclusively in some of the poorest sectors of the world economy — like India, Malawi, Ecuador, Tunisia, Ethiopia — that Achievement motivation can be developed so that those who have been through training become more active and suc-cessful small business people. Closer to home we have demon-strated that week-long seminars are effective in improving man-agement performance if they deal openly with feedback to partic-ipants as to their standing on various competencies that are need-ed for the work they are engaged in. In one case we found that such seminars for managers enabled them to change in significant enough ways for sales of the units they managed to increase dra-matically in the following year (Burnham and McClelland HBR article, Jan–Feb 1995).

Furthermore, Boyatzis and his colleagues* have been carrying out extensive studies at the Weatherhead School of Management at

---

* Boyatzis, RF, Cowen, SS, Kolb, DA and Associates (1995) *Innovation in professional education: Steps on a journey from teaching to learning*, Jossey-Bass, San Francisco, CA.

Case Western Reserve which show that if students get feedback early on what competencies they need in greater strength and set goals to acquire them, then two years later there is significant improvement in the competencies they set out to acquire. So one source of people with desired competencies is from the graduates of this school who have not only received regular business training, but also training in development of competencies needed in business.

Finally, in a study of executives in a large multinational company, we found that simply providing them with the knowledge of which competencies were associated with success on the job, feedback as to where they stood on these competencies, and with an opportunity to make plans for improvement, their performance did improve in the coming year. There were also significantly fewer people who left the company — which saved the company a lot of money. There are even individualised guidebooks available to help people develop the competencies they need through exercises or courses they pursue in their own time.

So business provides worthwhile goods and services through people working together. Plans and work designs help them to understand how their work fits together but such plans only work well if the people involved in them have the competencies that go with performing such jobs well. Identifying people with those competencies and putting them in place is an important first step, but it often works just as well to train people to develop the competencies they need for the work they are doing.

People with the right competencies in the right jobs means competitive advantage, producing better profitability which serves the ultimate goals of a good business — to maximise the satisfaction of the owners, producers and customers!

Introduction

Nick Boulter and Jackie Hill

For many years, eminent researchers have tried to identify what it is about an individual that makes them perform well in a work situation. As recently as 1994, Murray and Herrnstein[1] once again raised the idea, argued by Brigham[2] in 1923, that competent performance is largely determined by inherited intelligence. Vast numbers of intelligence and aptitude tests are still in general use for recruitment and selection, even though it has been proved time and time again that there is little correlation between the results of these tests and the performance of the individual once they are doing the job.

This book is about building competitive advantage through people. It is about how companies can make major business breakthroughs, how they can out-perform their competition, through focusing on better managing their people. And the book gives straightforward illustrations of what every company can do to improve its performance.

The book is about competencies — looking at the way people behave as a predictor of performance, rather than straight intelligence or aptitude scores. Competencies are also about indicators of performance in the work place, not in the examination room.[3] Decades of research have proven that past behaviour is the best

---

1 Murray, C, and Herrnstein, R (1994) *The Bell Curve*, New York.
2 Brigham, CC (1923) *A Study of American Intelligence*, Princeton, Princeton University Press.
3 McClelland, DC (1973) Testing for competence rather than for 'intelligence', *American Psychologist*, 28, 2–14.

predictor of future behaviour, so competencies are usually assessed through interviews which probe how the interviewee actually behaved in certain past work-related events. This book contains descriptions and examples of the interview techniques used, and how the resulting information can be used to determine what competencies are required in a particular role and whether an individual has those competencies.

This book also covers the various applications to which competencies can be applied and illustrates these through case studies of work conducted with a wide range of clients.

If you are a line manager, you may have already noticed that more and more of the traditional HR issues are coming your way as organisations de-centralise and corporate functions such as HR are either out-sourced or responsibilities passed to other areas. This book will help you to understand how you can use competencies, either for your own processes and procedures or liaising with your HR function, to enhance the calibre and performance of your people: how you can build a high performing team.

If you are a Human Resources professional, you will find this book an invaluable tool in understanding how your organisation can use competencies to better recruit, select and develop the best performers: how you can deliver programmes that have very positive business results.

All of the Hay/McBer methods, tools and techniques mentioned in this book are based on solid academic research and extensive fieldwork. Hay/McBer is part of the HayGroup – the leading consultancy helping organisations realise their strategies through their people.

Hay/McBer would like to thank all of those organisations who contributed their case studies and success stories. We would also like to thank Tjerk Hooghiemstra for helping instigate this book: Tjerk was European Practice Director for Hay/McBer in Europe, and is now a Human Resources Director at Philips.

1

Building Competitive Advantage Through People

Murray Dalziel

WHAT IS IN THIS BOOK FOR YOU?

This book is about realising strategy through people. The business environment in which we carry out change has itself changed dramatically in recent years and continues to do so at an ever increasing pace. This means that managers increasingly need tools to help them make change happen, and the greatest change agents are people.

In the 1980s, we carried out research for a number of companies on the human factors that promoted change. Recently this work was reviewed to identify the major differences between the 1980s and the 1990s. One issue remains the same. It does not matter how brilliant your ideas are, or your technology, the critical success factors in change revolve around people. What has changed is that today's initiatives are broader and more far reaching.

In the early 1980s, the challenge was to introduce a particular technology, or a single programme. You might have introduced computers into engineering, or the manufacturing process, but these would have been separate initiatives. By the late 1980s the challenge was to make sure that the introduction of these new technologies was linked in some way. The implication was that these changes would affect how work gets done.

In the 1990s, we are questioning how and indeed why everything is done. Do you really need the engineering function in the first place? We used to advise clients to pilot change to get experience. Today, this is not possible. By the time you have piloted the change, some other business change has occurred to make the programme at best inappropriate, at worst completely redundant. Recognising this, business process re-engineering was developed. How many business process re-engineering efforts have, in your experience, really delivered the promised benefits? Are you in an organisation where there is more than one change programme running, and you are wondering how the people in your organisation are going to take it all in?

Are you a senior line manager? Do you wonder why your visions of change get stuck somewhere in the organisation? You cannot quite put your finger on it but change is definitely not moving as fast as you would like.

Perhaps you are a human resources director and you know you need to re-focus some of the basic programmes in your organisation to support change. Naturally you are a bit apprehensive about this. You do not want to throw away well-established programmes just for the sake of change. After all, great ideas about compensation must still be backed up by payroll cheques and people still have to be recruited and trained.

As a human resources manager or specialist, you may be wondering how your area of responsibility fits into the overall change effort.

In this book, we aim to give you a framework to enable the people in your organisation to become really effective and for you to understand your personal contribution to your company's change programme. Do not expect any earth-shatteringly new theories. Much of this may not be new to you, because our research, from which the framework has been devised, is based on observations of what the most successful companies are doing to make their strategies work through their people. Many of these companies are represented in case studies throughout this book.

CHANGE IS CONSTANT – AND FAST

How many times have you heard that 'change is constant, and has always been'? This is true, but the pace of change is much faster today. When history books are written in a hundred years or so, the 1980s and 1990s will be looked on as another industrial revolution. The very nature of work itself is undergoing fundamental change and, like most advances, made possible by new technology.

Talk to any parent who worked in insurance who now has a son or daughter working in the same industry. The one thing they do not talk about is insurance. It is not only that many of the companies that the parent used to deal with are no longer in existence (there has been so much restructuring), or the fact that many ways of selling insurance were not available ten years ago (buying and selling insurance in banks, or over the telephone). The real reason that the parent and the son or daughter have so little in common is because the way in which work gets done is being revolutionised. When it comes to jobs in the industry, they do not speak the same language. Yet this is an industry that has been slower than many to grab the possibilities that technology has contributed to change.

And it is the same in other industries. Take the motor industry for example. Automation has already radically changed jobs in manufacturing. Now they are changing on the sales floor. Customers will no longer have to wander around models standing in the show room, then bargain with the salesperson about model, colour, delivery date and price. Soon you will be able to construct a model of your choice on the computer display in the salesroom and have the date of delivery confirmed then and there (in ten days, 90% of the time, according to one motor company).

BLUEPRINTS AND THE REAL NATURE OF WORK

Many senior managers, and you may be among them, are uncomfortable with change. It is fast, necessary, inspiring – but it does not always work. A familiar scenario is illustrated by the following example. At a recent board meeting, a non-executive director asked the chairman why they had not been completely successful in making change happen in one of their critical divisions, despite all the creative strategic thinking and critical changes in top management. The chairman told him that what he had failed to foresee was the inability of people in the middle of the organisation to identify what had to be done. He went on to say that it was not middle management resistance that had frustrated change efforts, as he and other senior managers had agreed the blueprints for change. It was that they had not realised the myriad details that need to be faced up to, to ensure the required change took place.

Blueprints are necessary but underneath the blueprints you have to see what work is really all about and how the skills themselves change. Ignoring these details places you at significant risk when implementing change.

The chapters in this book describe the Hay/McBer method, tools and techniques, based on solid academic research and extensive fieldwork, and give case studies to help you understand how you can use these tools to realise the changes you require through your people.

WHAT THIS MEANS FOR THE HUMAN RESOURCES AGENDA

What is coming through clear and strong is that people are the critical success factors for change. Historically that link has been weak. Senior management has simply not seen the link between people and bottom line business results. Chapter 2 looks into why this has been the case and introduces a powerful tool for making the link in your business. If the changes to work and people are so fundamental, what radical changes does that imply for the way in which companies manage their human resources? The companies with the most successful change management are those that retain their familiar and basic human resources programmes, but in addition they convert them into powerful new tools to manage the central aspects of change.

There are three main building blocks for change. Firstly you must know the direction in which you are going, **clarity**; secondly have the **commitment** to make it happen and thirdly, have the people with the required skills, **capability**. It all seems obvious – but well over half of change efforts fail due to lack of proper consideration for one or more of these three elements. Successful organisations link these three building blocks with three key ingredients of the human resources agenda: leadership, reward and role design.

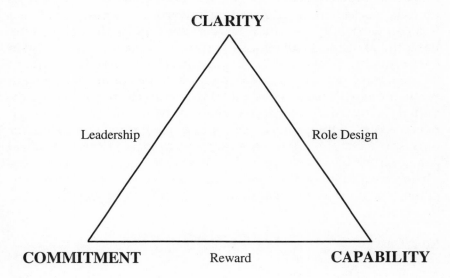

Leadership

Clarity and focus are two of the greatest change elements. You also need leaders who can make the link between where you want to go and peoples' commitment to get there. In other words, leaders who have the ability to build a motivated workforce. How do you ensure that the managers in your business have the capabilities to lead major change?

Chapter 4 discusses the key findings of our 1995 study into what differentiates outstanding international CEOs from the rest. It describes the competencies involved and what they look like.

Chapter 5 goes on to describe a particular example where competencies were developed to enable one of the world's most successful firms to develop the very best senior managers.

Reward and Recognition

Reward and recognition are often overlooked as levers for change in organisations. Too many businesses see reward as the last element that should be changed. We recognise that there are all sorts of risks associated with changing reward strategies, but unless you can work out how you reward and recognise the people who have the skills and capabilities you need, then it is hard to gain commitment. A change of pay by itself will not bring about change, but how can you expect people to be committed to team work and have a team focus if all the incentives are based on individuals? You cannot expect people to work in totally re-engineered roles, deploy more skills and work harder and better for only small increments to base pay and modest bonuses. Radical change must be accompanied by radical changes in the way people are rewarded and recognised. Chapter 9 discusses why competencies should be related to pay, and the practical issues involved.

Role Design

A large retail bank wanted to catch up on a competitor which had already successfully launched a telephone banking operation. It had the best in telecommunications and computer equipment to support it. It developed profiles of the people who were good on the telephone and hired people to match the profiles either from its branches or from other organisations which had a longer history of telephone sales and service. Having done this, the results were disappointing.

The top executives decided that their selection standards must have been wrong. What we found when we worked with them, however, was more complicated than that. They had actually hired two different types of people: one group was of people who had many of the necessary competencies needed to deliver good service to customers, the other group's members were focused on selling over the telephone. The problem was that the roles were confused. The question was 'was this a unit specifically set up to focus on selling products over the telephone, or was it set up to provide a special range of banking services?'. This was important as the 'hard' telephone salespeople found some of the service aspects extremely frustrating.

The two groups have radically different competencies. Direct sellers have a drive for results, low fear of rejection and an ability to listen and respond. The best service providers have a drive for improvement, customer service focus, visual empathy (they built a picture in their minds of the person on the other end of the line), and the ability to listen and respond. They only had this last competency in common. Confused roles is a common pitfall in business re-engineering. Work is, correctly, designed from the point of view of customer needs, but the objective is not then linked to the current capabilities or those being recruited for. For this telephone banking group, the roles were not clearly and correctly defined, the capabilities became confused and in order to rectify the problem, they had to start recruitment all over again. Chapter 3 describes what competencies are and how value can be created through competency-based human resources management. Chapter 6 is an illustration using a case study of competency-based assessment and selection in a company that needs over 100 new executives a year to meet its growth objectives.

A fourth key building block is coherence. Senior managers need to ensure that the individual change programmes fit in with the organisation as a whole. Many organisations have long shopping lists of change programmes running at the same time and many employees find it difficult to see how they will all come together. There are three key ingredients for human resource management that successful organisations use to build coherence. These are culture shaping, performance management and job/person matching.

Culture Shaping

Culture shaping is often misunderstood, so an example may help here. A service company wanted to change direction. It had a rea-

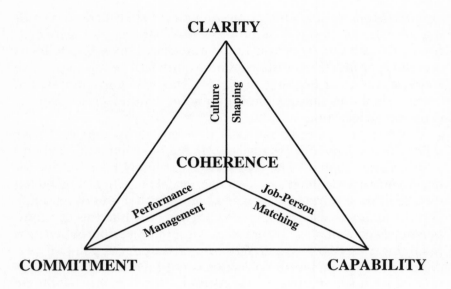

CLARITY

COHERENCE

Culture Shaping

Performance Management

Job-Person Matching

COMMITMENT   CAPABILITY

sonably good history of performance in its segment but wanted to re-examine its fundamental processes and map out a world-wide change strategy. As part of this initiative, it sponsored a study to compare its culture with that of the brand leader for its particular industry. They made a surprising discovery. One of the key differences, and potentially the reason that they could recruit and retain the sort of talent they needed was because they gave their people great freedom to act when dealing with a client. At the same time, this freedom was being challenged by new processes such as the world wide client reporting and management system. Whilst the change programme meant that fundamental changes were needed in many of their existing systems, through this study the organisation was able to recognise that building in that freedom to act, so valued by the people working in the organisation, gave them a source of competitive advantage when it came to recruitment and retention.

Many organisations spend time and effort on the 'values' they want the business to embrace, but what underlies the culture of an organisation are the beliefs and actions of the people in it. Just as competencies explain what underlies individual performance, culture shaping explains what underlies company performance. Chapter 7 discusses managing the environment in which people can optimally develop their competencies, how motivation and job requirements need to be matched for success and the management styles that impact organisational climate.

Performance Management

Top performing companies also use performance management to build coherence. Most organisations are familiar with the mechanics of performance management, but the organisations that make it work are the ones with an intense drive for results. It starts with leadership and extends to the whole business. Managers who do not have a fundamental drive for improving and beating standards of excellence cannot make performance management work. New systems based on teams may be leading edge, but are irrelevant without this fundamental drive for results. Human resources departments invest in new forms for objective setting and appraisal, but these are not enough if they do not also help to acquire and develop managers with a drive for results.

There are two trends in making performance management work. Firstly, moving from annual goal setting and appraisal as the sole vehicle for delivering performance management to a 90 day agendas for individuals and teams. Secondly, 360 degree feedback is becoming popular even in those cultures where previously people found it difficult to give feedback at all. Our recent research suggests that 360 degree feedback needs to be used with caution. The 360 degree ratings were compared with measurements of the same people's competencies taken from an intensive interview that was part of an assessment centre. It was found that if the 360 degree ratings were based on a proven competency model, then they could distinguish who was a top performer and who needed development (just as the interviews could). It was difficult however, to distinguish which particular competency it was that singled out top performers. In 360 ratings, if you are good, you tend to get good ratings overall. This is fine if you want to pay people on the basis of ratings, but not so good for development. The most pragmatic thing to do is to use the 360 degree rating system as a way of setting goals in those areas which affect other people, in delegation and coaching for example. Chapter 8 describes how performance management is changing from an appraisal approach to more development and coaching, and why the appropriate use of competency models is becoming more important in today's business environment.

People/job Matching

In the aftermath of large scale change, many people are looking to 're-select' their people to fit the new work. The sales person who was marvellous at calling on 50 corner shops may not be able to work in a team that devises and executes strategies to penetrate a chain of hypermarkets. Many organisations use assessment centres, or other formal methods, but there are also organisations which spend millions restructuring and putting in new business systems, then redeploy people on the basis of gut feel and then wonder why they do not see the expected benefits of the change.

One place where this is absolutely critical is in shaping the way top managers think about their jobs as a result of change. One of the manufacturing organisations that we work with has a huge commitment to change. It has spent $25 million a year for the past few years in modernisation; every piece of equipment on the 235,000 square foot facility has been reconfigured and every process re-thought. The manufacturing director can explain the teams, the team leaders, the decisions people make on their own, the fact that the people are involved in things like the hiring process and when to work overtime, how they can stop the line and call for and execute all the line changes. He can explain about continuous flow, one-piece-at-a-time production, the pull system, management by sight, housekeeping and quality, about the difference between articulation and realisation, about mind-set. The vision is clear. Charts are posted everywhere throughout the plant, the data recorded there is by the teams themselves. Everyone knows what is going on. Information has become a fuel as well as a tool.

When we asked the manufacturing director 'What do you do?', he stopped for a moment, thinking. It is almost as though he has not given it much thought before.

'I advise', he finally says. 'I mentor. I give feedback.'

'You don't manage?'

'The teams and the team leaders do that' he replies. 'I couldn't possibly manage all that's going on out here. And even if I could manage everything, could solve things for everyone, could wrap up problems in neat little solutions, why would I want to? That's what they know, what they do. That's their lives.'

At senior levels, despite change, many of the roles keep the same portfolio of responsibilities and the same job titles. You would have thought that there would be little change to the manufacturing director's job in the example above, but there are fundamental differences about what is required for managers to be successful. These differences have little to do with tasks or accountabilities and everything to do with thinking differently: their work, the customer, the management style of direct reports and fostering new work styles across the organisation. These require new competencies. Matching senior managers to new competencies is as important as ensuring that people further down the organisation can ultimately do the work. This is also not simply a one-off change. Recruitment and selection processes need to change to seek out and identify competencies for the new management required.

Chapters 10 and 11 describe various tools that you can use to improve recruitment and selection. Chapter 12 contains a case study of a project at Levi Strauss where the target was to find the best match between employees and future jobs following a major redesign of the organisation.

In conclusion, three main combinations are necessary if you are to sustain change successfully:

- An ongoing organisational development strategy which combines culture shaping, role design and job/person matching.

- An ongoing performance development strategy which combines performance management, reward and job/person matching

- An ongoing leadership development strategy which combines culture shaping, leadership and performance management.

This book deals with the issue of building competitive advantage through people. It builds strongly on the our own methodologies and on experiences with clients who are realising their strategy through people.

We wish you success in your change efforts and in realising your strategies through your people.

2

Improving Organisational Performance: Aligning Corporate Strategy and the Management of People

Sylvia DeVoge and Chris Dyson

THE LINK BETWEEN BUSINESS RESULTS AND PEOPLE

Historically, senior management has not seen the link between people and bottom line business results. Annual reports are prepared with sentiments such as 'people are our most important asset' or that 'people are our source of competitive advantage,' but many of these same organisations are reluctant to spend time, money and energy on programmes which will help people to perform and contribute to their optimum level.

Companies which would not in their wildest dreams allow a major piece of capital equipment to go without repair, maintenance or upgrading allow their people assets to rust and deteriorate in their performance.

The problem is not dishonesty, nor a malicious, evil disregard for people. The problem is the failure to see the link between people and business results. It is based on a misguided view that 'strategy' or 'process' is more important than people.

Take as an example a large international organisation operating in the fast moving consumer goods industry. It is losing market share and profits are slipping. A study of its top 200 managers revealed significant weaknesses in absolute and in comparative terms against other high performing organisations. In brief:

- The top managers were singularly lacking in strategic direction, focusing the majority of their time on operational matters.

- The whole of the management population showed a notable and severe absence of follow-through on initiatives and programmes.

- There was a significant weakness in confronting performance issues, and almost a total absence of coaching or development activity.

When faced with this information the executive team acknowledged this was true — but was reluctant to devote time and resources to upgrade the managers. A leading executive in the company responded in this way: 'We have a significant performance gap in the market place which we have to resolve, we cannot afford the time and energy to spend on people! The *real* problem is that we do not have the right products.'

This shows how organisations see people as one or even two steps removed from business results. It is also a powerful example of why this thinking is wrong, and dangerous:

> *If the problem is lousy products then how did this happen? Surely people had a role in creating them in the first place, and in not upgrading them in the second place; and surely it is people who will have to innovate new products in the future.*

How do you achieve anything in business except through people? Whether the issue is one of poor capital equipment, inefficient distribution channels, ineffective marketing, or bad resource allocation, it *always* comes back to people.

INTEGRATED SOLUTIONS

The successful organisations of the future — those which secure a true competitive advantage — will be those which understand the link between their business results and people. By understanding this link, they will be able to vastly improve the performance of people in their organisation, and achieve in reality the propositions that 'people are our most important assets' and 'people are our source of competitive advantage.'

Understanding the link between people and business results does not require a leap of faith. However it does require a different kind of clarity about external strategic objectives, internal critical success factors, and 'people factors' or levers and integrated solutions. It also requires a different model or way of thinking from the one that many senior executives have been taught in the past.

This Business Benefits Trail (©) is a powerful way of making the link between people and results.

Without this clarity of thought, solutions stay one-dimensional and ignore the people aspects which are essential to making things happen.

In the example above, the organisation went straight from strategy (increase market share) to solution (new and better products).

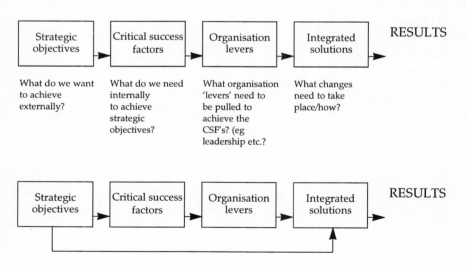

In doing so, they ignored some critical success factors such as:

- excellent market intelligence to understand consumer demands and trends;

- capability to innovate and translate into marketable products;

- fast time-to-market for new/revised products;

- good relationships with distribution channels.

By ignoring the critical success factors, there was no way for the company to make a quality assessment of which organisation levers needed to change, and how they needed to change to achieve the desired strategy. A review of this might have revealed something along the lines illustrated below:

Organisation lever	CSFs			
	Market intelligence	Innovation	Time to market	Distribution channels
Leadership	✔	✔		
Values & culture		✔✗		
Work processes	✔✗		✔✗	✔✗
Individual & team capabilities	✗	✔		
Organisation & job design		✔✗	✔✗	
Management processes	✗			
Reward		✔✗		
✔ = essential to achieving CSFs ✗ = Gap				

As a result there were major gaps between the changes needed, and their ability to achieve these.

Ultimately, all the organisation levers are activated or pulled by people. If there is no clarity about the organisation levers and how they relate to the critical success factors, there is no way to define what people need to do differently in order to achieve the desired strategy.

The organisation in our example had no such clarity and as a result its solution was one dimensional. There is a significant difference between implementing a solution which is 'new products', and implementing a solution which is based on critical success factors, and integrated around the relevant organisation levers which people can activate.

THE BUSINESS BENEFITS TRAIL

Making the link between business results and people is essential for organisations seeking to add value from their people in a strategic way.

Technically sound and elegant human resources programmes are not good enough. Whether it is a state-of-the art reward strategy, comprehensive management development, or competency based performance management, human resources programmes must now meet two requirements to be truly value adding and strategic:

- they must be integrated with the organisation's critical success factors;

- there must be a clear link with business benefits.

The Business Benefits Trail is explored in more detail in the sections below:

- when the starting point is the solution (ie at the end of the trail);

- when there are too many change initiatives on the go.

When the starting point is the solution

The starting point for many engaged in human resources management is at the end of the benefits trail — with a solution. But regardless of the starting point, it is essential to work back through the trail. Without a clear understanding of how human resources solutions relate to critical success factors and strategy, human resources programmes become disconnected from business results, and become ends in themselves — initiatives.

Example : a Global Energy Company

For one human resources function in a global energy company its starting point was the solution of a new reward strategy. Senior line managers wanted HR to re-vamp the pay strategy to bring it in line with the needs of the business: several years of downsizing, delayering and process redesign were accompanied by only tiny changes to the reward system. It was difficult to reward people in a flatter structure and pay-for-performance increments were seen as derisory. Everyone was clear about the solution but they did not understand how this linked to business benefits, or how this fitted with strategy or critical success factors.

The senior human resources managers worked with key line managers in a two day workshop to define the missing elements. At the end the human resources programme had changed from a single human resources solution for a new reward strategy to an integrated solution for:

- management development: to upgrade managers' skills and competencies in managing, coaching and developing people in a flatter organisation structure;

- succession planning: processes to manage people's expectations about potential career moves; career mapping based on competencies and skills;

- reward: revised incentive and bonus schemes, and processes for managing performance.

As a result the approaches adopted addressed many of the key 'people' issues together, in an integrated manner that was clearly solving business needs, rather than being an unconnected technical solution.

Example : an integrated Pharmaceutical organisation

In another example, the human resources function of an international pharmaceutical company had as its starting point a 'competency model for sales managers.' When working back through the trail, it became clear that the human resources programme needed to be much broader, to achieve the intended business result.

A key *strategic objective* was growth in European markets.

Critical success factors to achieve this were around distribution channels and sales capability.

Relevant organisation levers were work processes; management processes (in particular, performance management); organisation and job design (team based selling required in new markets); and individual and team capability (in particular, competencies).

The integrated solution did include competencies, but also involved sales process redesign; performance management reward systems, and job redesign. Linking the processes and the people issues to address the strategic need produced a far more effective result.

Too Many Change Initiatives at Once

Go to any company today and you will hear the same complaint: that there are too many initiatives on the go. In the majority of cases, the problem relates to the following:

- lack of clarity about how the initiatives relate to strategy and business results;

- lack of clarity about how the initiatives relate to each other;

- poor design — lack of integration.

All of these stem from failing to understand the Business Benefit Trail.

Example : A Large Bank

A UK based commercial bank found itself with 20 change programmes, all running concurrently. Management was getting overloaded and confused. The temptation was to begin by tackling the change programmes — keep what was needed and jettison what was not. But this should be the final step, *after* clarifying the strategic objectives, critical success factors and organisation levers. To illustrate this case, each step in the Business Benefits Trail is discussed in turn.

Strategic Objectives

Although the bank had done a considerable amount of work on strategy, the strategic objectives were not clear enough, and there were too many (approximately 15 in all). There were three major problems:

1. *Actions:* some of the strategic objectives were actually actions (eg 'acquire a company').

2. *Measures:* many of the objectives were measures (eg Earnings Per Share growth); measures are required to gauge success of achieving strategic objectives, but in themselves are not strategic objectives.

3. *Internal:* some strategic objectives were internally focused (eg 'improve management information system').

There were five strategic objectives, based around what they wanted to achieve externally with regard to:

- customers

- competitors

- stakeholders

- suppliers, and

- market image.

Critical Success Factors

The clarity of strategic objectives provided a solid foundation for defining the critical success factors. It was important to define the critical success factors in terms of *decided end-points* versus actions. For example, in one case, a critical success factor was changed from

'new IT system'

to

'capability to process 98% of customer queries with one call, within three minutes'

Whereas the critical success factors of 'new IT systems' is very narrow and leads only to a new IT system, the critical success factors 'capability to process 98% of customer queries with one call, within three minutes' is broader and leads to a new IT system *and many other things* (for instance job design and values) necessary to achieve the critical success factors.

Organisation Levers and Competitive Advantage

To understand, analyse and formulate integrated solutions there needs to be a model which divides an organisation in its component parts. A valid organisation model needs to be an open system.

It also needs to be comprehensive and yet readily understandable. One that is attractive and incorporates most of the features mentioned above is the Burke-Litwin model.

However, this model suffers from two problems:

- over complexity (simplicity is a key requirement);

- our research shows that one of the components (climate) that is included as an intervening variable is an output, or result.

Figure 2.1, the Hay Seven Lever Model of Integrated Organisation Change (©), is founded on research, it is an open system, it recognises the inter-relationship of all components, it is simple and, perhaps most importantly, we and our clients have found it extraordinarily valuable in supporting our understanding of managing change.

In the interest of common understanding around the world and the many languages in which we consult the definitions of the components have been kept succinct and perhaps simple. We consider this to be a worthwhile trade-off by ensuring common understanding. The definitions of the components are as follows:

- Realising Strategy Through People

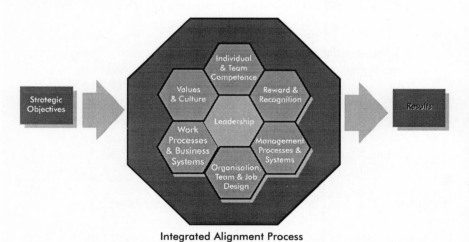

Integrated Alignment Process

Figure 2.1   Hay Seven Lever Model of Integrated Organisation Change ©

Strategic Intent
The organisation purpose, overall goals and the plans to achieve them.

Leadership
The ability of the leadership to mobilise the organisation around the strategy. (This component is central to the model both graphically and by intent).

Values and Culture
The way in which organisational norms support the strategy.

Work Processes and Business Systems
The sequence of activities through which resources are transformed to meet customer needs

Organisation, Team and Job Design
The way in which accountabilities are organised

Management Processes and Systems
The key processes through which management influences people.

Reward and Recognition
The manner in which behaviour, capability and/or results are reinforced.

Individual and Team Competence
The capability of people (individually and as a team) to carry out the strategy

Results
The business, societal and organisational climate outcomes from the integration and interaction of the organisation levers directed by the strategic intent.

It is more usual for two or more of the levers to be designed to interact from the outset of an intervention. There are also many occasions when after making a change in one sphere it has become apparent that there is a need to change other components of the model. For example a major international manufacturer of capital equipment had a strategic objective to grow its market share and to challenge the leading player in the market. It had concluded that any further growth by acquisition would be likely to be challenged as reducing competition therefore organic growth was to be the route to meeting the strategic objective.

The client had recognised that the quality of its sales force was variable and generally was not of as good quality as that of the market leader. As a consequence the company wanted to improve the quality of its existing sales representatives, and to recruit better quality people to the role in future. It decided to take a competency approach to fulfilling these critical success factors for meeting the strategic objective.

During the course of the project it became clear that there was considerable variation across the world in the sales business process, there were significant differences in organisational structures and their effectiveness; and finally the quality of immediate management too was a major problem. Although the competency project to improve the quality of new recruits and to develop the capability of existing staff was going to add value, there would be significantly greater value to be gained by leveraging other components as well.

Individual and team competencies have a critical inter-relationship with leadership. Our research shows that leadership which articulates a clear and compelling vision and relates that vision to what each individual is required to contribute is a most potent lever for change.

Successful change

One example of a company with ongoing interventions using these two levers is Mobil Corporation which researched and developed a competency model for leaders in the company and supported the managers with development programmes to grow and enrich line management competencies. After a decade the Exceptional Manager Programme is still the cornerstone of Mobil's leadership development. An internal research project to measure the effectiveness of the intervention showed that managers who were participants and who consciously implemented their learning achieved a 20% improvement in the performance of their operating unit in comparison with their past performance and in comparison with colleagues who had not been involved or had not implemented their learning.

Another frequent link is between the competencies and values and culture levers. It is the behavioural manifestation of competencies that underlie the culture and values in action: the walk matching the talk. The Bank of Ireland linked the values and culture required by its business strategy not only to the competencies (or 'management practices' as they call them) required of high performing managers but also to the reward and recognition programmes and to the changes in management processes, especially performance management. The chief executive says that the programme has had a significant impact on the capabilities of management to solve the business challenges that lie ahead and to sustain an already successful performance.

A final example of the links that are inherent in any successful organisational change between competencies, organisation and job design and business processes is Sun Life Assurance Society.

The then managing director had missionary zeal and exemplary leadership capability. Following a review of strategy and high level restructuring to meet the new strategy, work was begun on the design of core processes. These new processes required a new focus on customers which in turn required a change in line managers' behaviours and the underlying values and culture of the business. The competencies and skills required of people in customer oriented teams were different from the past. The work and job structure was transformed. People who had previously performed only 25% of a process required new competencies and skills to undertake the other 75%. New reward structures based on pay for competencies and customer related performance measures were introduced.

The hard work of implementing these changes and carefully linking them was not in vain. Sun Life achieved 40 – 90% improvement in process turnaround times, 10% reduction in unit costs and 50–80% quality improvements (right first time). The change in style of management leadership was also a successful outcome of the major change interventions.

Business results
This chapter's purpose has been to set a context within which competencies interventions sit. We have also made the link between

intervention and the business benefits to be derived. We urge you to expect and demand significant business benefit from any organisational intervention. We need to recognise, from the outset, that pulling only one of the organisational change levers alone will rarely reap the potential return on investment that is possible if all the inter-relationships are explored and exploited.

3

Why are Some People More Successful than Others?

Patricia Marshall

In recent years a number of studies have been carried out to try to understand why some people are successful in life and others are not. Psychologists have investigated the lack of positive correlation between IQ and success at work and in personal relationships. The brightest and the best do not always succeed, so how can we predict who will succeed and make the best choices about people and jobs?

Organisations are changing and the pace of change is perceived to be accelerating. Whether or not this is true, the perception creates problems for both organisations and individuals within them. But problems, as the English writer, GK Chesterton put it, are only adventures wrongly construed. In this chapter we shall look at how Hay/McBer has turned the problem of how to get the right match between people and jobs into an adventure with a happy – and productive – ending.

David McClelland published an article in 1973 entitled 'Testing for competence rather than for intelligence'.[1] In this paper McClelland summarised a number of studies which showed that aptitude tests which had traditionally been used by psychologists to predict performance did not work:

---

[1] McClelland, DC (1973), 'Testing for Competence Rather Than for Intelligence', *American Psychologist*, 28, 1–14.

- They were not predictive of job performance;

- Tests were often culturally based and therefore prone to bias;

- Other measures such as examination results and references were equally poor at predicting success.

We have probably all known someone at work, an excellent performer in his or her current role, who is promoted and does not succeed in the new job. They have not lost their expertise or their wits, something else has happened. Or we may know people who could do an excellent job but are not considered because they have no formal qualifications. Prejudices may be racial, give poor results for one gender or another or act against minority groups or certain socio-economic groups. These biases are not just unfair to the people affected, they are also bad for the organisation as they may rule out people who would have been able to do the job well had they been selected. People within the organisation could leave because they were not considered for promotion. This is a real loss both in terms of the talent walking out of the door and because of the impression given by the organisation to other employees.

McClelland set out to find an alternative to the traditional aptitude and intelligence testing, and it was these alternative variables that he labeled competency. McClelland's approach to finding competencies which would predict performance included two methods:

- The use of criterion samples;

- The use of what is now called a behavioural event interview to identify the thought and behaviour patterns of people who are successful in the jobs being studied.

These methods, which proved to be highly successful in predicting future success of individuals, are the foundations of the Hay/McBer methodology. They are elegant in their conceptual simplicity. The basis of the method is that to know what creates success in a job then one needs to make a comparison of what the best performers are doing in comparison with average performers – criterion groups. To understand what makes the best people successful we need to understand not just what they do, but the thoughts and feelings which generate their actions. Doing this gives access to what would otherwise be hidden characteristics which are important drivers of behaviour delivering excellent performance. This is done through the behavioural event interview (BEI). This is a structured form of critical incident interview which focuses on the characteristics of the person being interviewed rather than on the work content.

WHAT IS A COMPETENCY?

A competency is an underlying characteristic of a person which enables them to deliver superior performance in a given job, role or situation. The iceberg model, as shown in the diagram below, shows different levels of competency.

Skills are things that people can do well, for example programming.

Knowledge is what a person knows about a specific topic, for example a computer language.

Social role is the image that an individual displays in public; it represents what he or she thinks is important. It reflects the values of the person, for example being a good employee, or a leader.

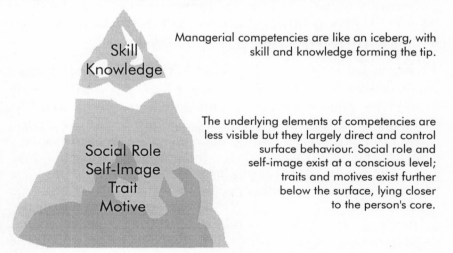

Skill
Knowledge

Managerial competencies are like an iceberg, with skill and knowledge forming the tip.

Social Role
Self-Image
Trait
Motive

The underlying elements of competencies are less visible but they largely direct and control surface behaviour. Social role and self-image exist at a conscious level; traits and motives exist further below the surface, lying closer to the person's core.

Figure 3.1 The Iceberg Model of Managerial Competencies

Self-image is the view people have of themselves. It reflects their identity, for example seeing oneself as an expert.

Traits are enduring characteristics of people. They reflect the way in which we tend to describe people. For example she is reliable, or he is adaptable. These characteristics are habitual behaviours by which we recognise people.

Motives are unconscious thoughts and preferences which drive behaviour because the behaviours are a source of satisfaction. For example, achievement drive, wanting to do better.

It is important to distinguish the different levels because they have significant implications for HR planning. For example, the top levels – skill and knowledge – are generally easier to train and develop, whereas those below the surface are more difficult to develop. It makes more sense to recruit or select for these competencies than to try to train people for them in the short term. It is, however, possible to develop them over a longer period by planning job moves for people which will give them the opportunity to develop characteristics which will be important in later, more senior roles. In addition, the more complex the job or role, the more likely it is that the very best performance is driven by the characteristics which are at the lower levels in the iceberg rather than task-related skills and knowledge at the top. Selecting on the basis of qualification or skill is therefore not going to help choose the very best performers in these jobs.

Many readers will have seen the results of promoting the best salesperson or the best engineer to a managing role with extremely poor results, often resulting in an unhappy employee as well. The characteristics which delivered best performance as a salesperson or engineer do not necessarily make for great performance as a manager and may positively get in the way, for example the drive personally to beat targets or produce the best designs will interfere with delivering through other people – which is what the manager has to do.

Some organisations which undertake competency studies stop at the level of describing behaviour. This does not give the full picture and can be misleading. For a behaviour to be truly a competency it needs to be associated with **intent,** ie the intentional use of behaviour in delivering a performance outcome. Behaviours may include thoughts, where the thought leads to behaviour which in turn delivers desired outcomes. In defining what we mean by competency we need to look at two major categories:

- Threshold competencies;
- Differentiating competencies.

Threshold competencies are the characteristics which any job holder needs to have to do that job effectively – but do not distinguish the average from superior performer. For example product knowledge or computational skill in an insurance salesperson.

Differentiating competencies are those characteristics which superior performers have but are not present in average performers. An example for an insurance salesperson may be customer service orientation: being able to put themselves in the shoes of the potential buyer of the products.

THE BENEFITS OF A COMPETENCY-BASED APPROACH

This approach has as its frame of reference the performance of the very best people in the job. The characteristics of these people provide a template for a number of human resource management processes: selection, development, succession planning, performance management, promotion and career-pathing. By improving the selection successes, by shifting people from average to superior performance through development and by promoting the right people, organisations can improve their overall productivity.

There has been a vogue recently for competency models and some organisations have wanted to created models for their own sake. We do not believe that models created under such circumstances can add much value and may be costly errors. A competency model by itself is a solution looking for a problem and therefore not a good starting point. Competency models produce great competitive advantage when they are part of the delivery of the business strategy. A company which wants to increase its market share by getting more from its current employees and hiring the best in the outside market will gain a great deal in bottom line savings from an accurately defined model of superior performance. This review of strategic direction and its effects on the business area concerned is a prerequisite to competency modeling.

STAGES OF COMPETENCY DEFINITION

There are six stages in defining a competency model for a given job or role. The content of the phases may vary depending on the depth of research required but omission of one of the stages will usually give poor results and may lead to a waste of investment. The stages are:

1. Clarify the performance criteria.

2. Identify people for the criterion samples.

3. Collect data through BEIs and/or other methods.

4. Analyse data and define the competencies.

5. Validate the model.

6 Design applications.

1. Performance criteria

Establishing the performance criteria at the outset of the project is critical. It is normal to establish a steering group to manage the project and its members should be in agreement about the criteria for superior performance for the job or role. It is only against this backcloth that the sample of average and outstanding performers chosen for the BEIs and the right competencies can be identified. The criteria should include hard data if possible, eg, productivity figures, but other criteria such as managerial effectiveness as measured by direct reports or peer ratings may be included. A single measure should be avoided.

Competency Research

Work Plan

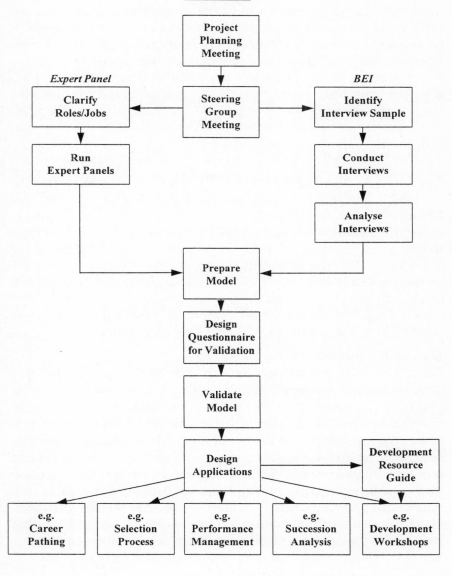

2. Criterion sample

In selecting people for the sample three things are important: the outstanding performers should be the absolute best, those who are rated high on all or most of the performance criteria; there needs to be a **control** or **contrast** group of fully acceptable performers, third-ly, the samples should be large enough to allow statistical analysis. A 10% sample should allow this but if the total population is small a higher proportion will be needed. A rule of thumb is to weight the sample towards a higher proportion of superior performers: 'you always learn most from your superstars'.[2]

3. Data collection

The data collection may be through BEIs or through other methods, the most common of which are expert panels or focus groups. The BEI method is the most effective but it is time consuming and needs expert interviewers to conduct the interviews, and expert analysts to interpret the results. Nonetheless it gives the best results and for key jobs or complex roles it is worth the investment. The results provide not only the competencies but also give rich data about the context in which the competencies are displayed and how they operate together, thus providing valuable information which can be used in helping others to develop the competencies.

Behavioural event interviews
The behavioural event interview is a form of structured interview similar to a critical incident interview but focused on the individual and their competencies rather than on the tasks. It is a process for indirectly collecting samples of behaviour which have led to suc-cess in the role the person has, and events where he or she has been frustrated in delivering what they wanted to do. The interview requires a high degree of rigour from the interviewer and — if done well — will reveal patterns of intentional behaviour which deliver outstanding performance. The interview focuses on thoughts, feel-ings behaviours and outcomes. A comparison of all the outstanding performers yields an excellent view of how they deliver against the

---

[2] Spencer, Lyle M & Spencer, Signe M (1993) *Competence at Work*, John Wiley & Sons Inc.

performance criteria and, when contrasted with average performers, results in a template of excellent performance in that particular role or job and which is specific to the organisation.

Expert panels
Expert panels or focus groups use people who are knowledgeable about the job — including outstanding job holders, customers, HR specialists and line managers. The panel brainstorms the competencies needed to do the job in an outstanding way. The panel needs good support so that it does not produce either over-generalised competencies (motherhood statements), or is dominated by people other than the job-holders. Panels typically do not generate the full range of competencies, in particular they may miss some of the thinking or motivational competencies. In general panels get about 50% accuracy when compared with BEI data, and tend to omit some of the unique competencies needed for a role.

Surveys
Another method of data collection is through surveys, either bespoke[3] or generic. While this is a quick way of generating a lot of data from many people it is limited in that you only get responses to the questions asked and, like expert panels, surveys will miss the hidden competencies which are often unique to the job or the organisation. Conducting a few BEIs to augment the data collected from panels or by surveys will improve the outcome but not provide the richness of a model created from a larger number of BEIs.

4. Data analysis and model development

Creating the models from BEIs is the most complex part of the process. The BEIs need to be analysed in a thematic way, ie in clusters according to themes related to patterns which are discernable in the BEIs, to generate hypotheses on what the competencies are and how they work together to produce outstanding performance. Comparison of what average people do and what outstanding performers do is the central part and, if the two groups have been cho-

---

[3] Surveys to develop competency models need to identify the behaviours and characteristics of the job holder, not the tasks they perform. The survey items should be short and unambiguous.

sen well against the criteria, then the differences often stand out. The analysis of the data is usually through both a thematic analysis of the interviews and using statistics to test for real differences between the two groups. Spencer and Spencer give a detailed account of this process in *Competence at Work*.[4]

The output may take the form of a competency dictionary which includes all the competencies, their definitions and definitions of the levels expressed as interval scales together with behavioural examples of the competency. The format depends on the nature of the applications for which the model will be used.

5. Validation

There are several ways to validate the model. It may be possible where there are large numbers of job-holders to create questionnaires based on the model and to administer them to a wider sample of job-holders. This includes both average and star performers. The analysis of this data will test the model and allow revisions and refinements to take place. Where there are not large enough numbers for this testing to take place then we recommend that data gathered as part of selection processes or performance reviews should be kept under review to use this as a mechanism for validating and updating the model. This data collection is important, particularly as jobs are not static and, as situations and jobs change and evolve, the competency framework will also have to be changed to reflect the new requirements. Often the competencies themselves do not change: the underlying motivational aspects of the jobs and people may remain constant, but the way in which the behaviours reflect the underlying drives may change.

6. Applications

Although this is the last phase in the development of a competency, it needs to be built into the thinking at an earlier stage. The form which the competency model takes and the content of the dictionary depends on what the intended use is. For example, if the model is to be used for selection, the selector may need to have

---

4 Spencer, Lyle M & Spencer, Signe M. Op. Cit.

examples of competencies which are difficult to develop and therefore make selection decisions made on these. Selectors need to understand the difference between threshold competencies which a person needs to do the job at all, and differentiator competencies which distinguish potentially average from potentially outstanding performers. The different applications may require different formats for the competencies and they can be rewritten in a variety of ways. For performance management, for example, the competencies may be most helpfully presented in a way which links them to specific deliverables. This can be powerful in helping people see that a lack of a certain competency or set of competencies gets in the way of their overall performance. It can then become a focus for development.

COMPETENCIES FOR THE FUTURE

What has been described are methodologies to define competencies in existing jobs. So how can we define what will work in the future – for new or fast developing roles?

The best approach is to look for similar jobs elsewhere – if they exist. This does not have to be in the organisation for which the competencies are being defined. It is possible to conduct interviews with outstanding performers in other organisations. In such studies it is important to look at the deeper competencies, the motives and the cognitive or thinking patterns of those in the study, rather than the superficial behaviours. This also works where managers do not believe they have star performers in their own organisation. The choice of organisation and job-incumbent needs to be managed with great care to ensure that the performance criteria give a good match. This is especially important given the variety of jobs which appear under the same title but which may have little real resemblance beyond the name.

A second approach to looking at new jobs is to define the separate elements of the job and to look for jobs which reflect those elements conducting BEIs and expert panels around those elements will provide a good basis for a model when the elements are merged.

A third approach is to focus on the environment in which these jobs will be performed, what will be different from now, and the competencies that will be most important to success.

CREATING VALUE

The value of a competency-based approach depends on a number of factors:

- the degree to which the competency study is based on the strategic needs of the organisation;

- the clarity with which the role or job is defined in relation to strategy;

- the rigour of the process used in defining the competencies;

- the care taken in determining the best assessments for the job-person matching process, whether it is for selection, succession planning, development or performance management.

The value can be measured in cost-saving, increased productivity, lower staff turnover because employees are better matched to jobs, reduced learning curves and therefore earlier higher productivity of new people.

4

Worldwide Leadership Differences

John B Larrere

Spanish explorer Ponce DeLeon was looking for the fountain of youth. He found Florida instead. Organisations for many years have looked for a single, magic set of competencies for their executives that will ensure good leadership and financial success. In looking for this 'fountain of leadership' they may find a nice place to visit like Florida, but they will be missing what it takes to be successful in the world at large.

A WORLD OF DIFFERENCE

Even within the same industry, the world of competencies is not singular but different. The challenges of driving an oil company, for example, whose orientation is exploration and production are different from the challenges for a down stream oil company which must focus and excel at marketing and refining. These orientations not only demand a different focus but result in unique cultures — cultures that are made more unique when one is predominantly British and another North American. These factors create a different context and a different set of demands that must be met to be successful.

In the oil industry, exploration and production need a longer time horizon for planning, developing concepts and strategy. They require peering into the future 15 to 25 years ahead, because decisions made today will have consequences then. Extracting natural resources requires creating partnerships with nations through their political and business leaders. To meet on equal terms with the powerful demands an ability to play on a large stage, to think in hugely complex ways and make far reaching decisions.

Marketing and refining rewards not only those who plan ahead but those who are able to recognise and seize opportunities. Planning ahead puts refineries on line that can process all different kinds of crude oil. Seizing the opportunity in a down stream oil company demands using market forces and trends to be able to obtain and refine the most cost effective mix of different crude oils.

COMPETENCIES ARE SITUATIONAL

The definition of a competency states that behaviour is a function of the person and the situation they find themselves in. The behaviour of a person flows from some characteristic of that person in conjunction with the situation in which they find themselves.

Behaviour = f (Person, Situation)

There are any number of situations that define the challenges and demands of a leader in the organisation. Being successful means matching the situation and the required behaviour. The wildcard in this match is the person's own competencies. People's own characteristics can help them match their behaviour to the situation or make it difficult for them to do what should be done in particular circumstances.

Different times and circumstances create a different set of situations. The insurance industry diverged in the late 1980s and early 1990s from its usual cyclical nature, suffering several down cycles in a row without intervening improvement. The times demanded cost containment and downsizing. A study conducted by LOMA (Life Office Management Association) and the Hay Group showed that these situations were handled best by a decisive, unilateral and coercive approach. In the same study, these behaviours were also shown to inhibit capital growth and revenue growth from first year premiums. A worldwide manufacturing organisation also found that using this same coercive style was effective at saving the organisation when it was in danger, but counterproductive when creativity was needed for revenue growth and market penetration.

People who are successful in one venue may have grave difficulty in another. Several Hay/McBer studies have revealed these key differences. They indicate that, although there are common or generic leadership competencies that are necessary for good performance in a variety of cultural, geographical and business situations, they are not sufficient to predict outstanding performance. In a meta analysis of several studies, David McClelland has found that the generic competencies do not explain enough variance in executive performance[1] to be reliable. But when these generic competencies are combined with unique competencies derived from particular situations and cultures, these competencies predict outstanding performance much more accurately.

GENERIC COMPETENCIES: COMMON GROUND

What are the common or generic competencies that are found in executives around the world? Global executives have in common three basic sets of competencies:

- competencies for sharpening the focus for their organisations;

- competencies for building commitment; and

- competencies for driving success.

Although these competencies seem to be sequential, in reality they occur simultaneously and in parallel as executives handle different situations.

FOCUS — THE HANDWRITING ON THE WALL

Finding focus is analogous to the ability of the biblical prophet Daniel 'to read the handwriting on the wall' (Dan 5:5-30). King

---

[1] The generic competencies correctly sort average and outstanding executives in terms of bottom line performance only 50% of the time. When the unique competencies are added 72% of typical and outstanding performers are correctly sorted.

Belshazzar held a feast during which 'the fingers of a man's hand appeared and wrote on the plaster of the wall of the king's palace, and the king saw the hand as it wrote. ... Then all the king's wise men came in but they could not read the writing or make known to the king the interpretation...Then Daniel was brought in before the king.' Daniel was asked to read it. He advised the king that his reign was in grave danger and he was right.

Successful executives around the world read the handwriting on the wall. They do broad scanning, ie, they gather information from a variety of sources, both formally — in conducting or commissioning research and informally by what they see, read and hear anecdotally. The best executives have cognitive flexibility which gives them decisive insight to interpret what they see, hear and learn in their broad scanning. This demands not just analytical thinking or conceptual thinking but an ability to move back and forth between the two modes of making sense of data. They are equally adept at creating their own hypotheses or personal rules of thumb from what they see in the market place as they are at dissecting a financial report.

The inability to move flexibly between these styles created difficulty. Those who were too conceptual were unable to understand the consequences of current decisions while those who were too

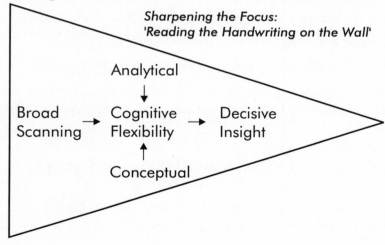

Figure 4.1 Reading the handwriting on the wall

analytical could not make sense of trends or recognise new paradigms emerging that would threaten their organisation.

Decades ago the then IBM CEO, Watson, saw that compatibility would be a technological and marketing advantage in the future. Where previously computers were built one at a time and were incompatible one with another, Watson bet substantial resources on making them compatible. He correctly read the handwriting on the wall and moved forward with decisive insight. To change the marketplace, Watson also had to build commitment in his organisation around this crucial approach.

BUILDING COMMITMENT

There are four competencies involved in building commitment: organisational know-how; good judgment of people; leadership; and impact and influence. More successful international CEOs exhibited high levels of these competencies than did those in a control group of US executives; and by wide margins: 22% to 10% for organisational know-how; 57% to 31% for impact and influence and 55% to 17% team leadership.

Organisational know-how is a combination of environmental scanning and understanding people and groups. Good judgment of people is a kind of executive maturity that allows people to size up the strengths and weaknesses of people and match them to tasks and to teams. With these two competencies, executives form teams in which the whole is greater than the sum of its parts. They understand people and how they interact to make outstanding, complex matches in building successful teams. Impact and influence is used to communicate well with people. These executives convey their values in a language that people can understand. By timing, choice of venue and influence strategies, they invite people to make their values and the executive's values converge. These executives help people experience how the best interest of the organisation and their own best interests are congruent: they gain commitment rather than compliance.

DRIVING FOR SUCCESS

Driving for success entails competencies that are common to successful entrepreneurs as well as successful leaders. The need to achieve energises executives to measure themselves and their organisations against a standard of excellence. They drive improvement, set challenging goals and take calculated entrepreneurial risks. They have an intuitive self confidence, ie, the courage of their convictions. In a study of CEOs of healthcare systems where key decisions had to be made on future alliances, mergers and acquisitions, the most successful readily cancelled deals that they felt lacked a necessary component, even when due-diligence indicated they should go forward with the deal.

Similarly, other executives moved forward without complete information to initiate projects or deals that they were convinced were advantageous and bold. The achievement drive and self confidence provided a self image as controller of his or her her own fate. This sense of efficacy led to initiating action. King Belshazzar's doom was already sealed by the time the prophet Daniel read the handwriting on the wall. Successful executives initiated action before events forced them to act.

The best executives see what others miss, provide a focus for their organisations, build the commitment of their organisations around their chosen focus and are not satisfied until they have exceeded their personal and organisational best. We would think that this would be enough to succeed; but some people who have had these executive competencies have failed when they moved from one organisation to another or from one culture to another or from one economic circumstance to another.

CRITICAL DIFFERENCES: IGNORE THEM
AT YOUR PERIL!

What are the key differences among successful executives that make them successful in one place and unsuccessful elsewhere? Our research has identified several enduring differences that spell success and failure. Motivation, time horizon, approach to business relationships, bias for action and the approach to exercising authority have spelt success and failure for executives worldwide:

Achievement	*Motive disposition*	Power
Short	*Time horizon*	Long
Personal	*Building business relationships*	Contractual
Planning	*Bias for action*	Implementation
Centralised	*Exercising authority*	Participatory

Motive Disposition

A motive disposition that spells success in AT&T or BP may not mean achieving the same success in a worldwide food business, the North American healthcare industry or Mobil. In a longitudinal study of management and leadership candidates conducted over 30 year period at AT&T, trainees who were tested for motive disposition at joining were tracked to see what level of leadership they attained over time. The history of the trainees showed that those with a high need for power were more likely to attain high leadership positions than those without it. Similarly, executives in IBM, Roman Catholic religious leaders, executives of BP and CEOs of successful life insurance companies were likely to share this ability to derive vicarious satisfaction from the success of people they work with. They are more likely to delegate, coach and develop others.

Organisational Structure, Products Affect Motive Requirements

Other organisations that are more decentralised or whose marketplace changes rapidly, are more likely to demonstrate achievement drive. This may be more common in organisations with a simpler product or range of products. Organisations that have complex products or product mixes, that have a need for international compatibility and synergy among products or organisational components, or where the satisfaction of success may be postponed for years to come for investments made today, are more likely to have executives who exhibit the power motive.

Behaviour that is intuitive, unconscious and successful in one organisation may be counterproductive in another. Being a bureaucratic player who can get various parties to work together may be both enjoyable and productive in the large complex organisation. That same bureaucratic ability may be ineffective in another because the situation does not warrant it: it adds little value in a marketplace with simple products and channels of distribution which rewards the quick and simple decision.

Time Horizon: What Does The Market Demand?

Elliott Jacques in *Requisite Organisation* has used the notion of time horizon to differentiate people. Complexity comes in both short term and long term doses, but Jacques notes that people demonstrate different abilities in the short term from those in the long term. Exploration and producing organisations and insurance organisations with complex, actuarially-driven revenue streams and future liabilities demand people who can conceptualise with long term horizons. Some market-driven organisations more often act with 90 day agendas than with 15 year time horizons. Executives differ in their ability to handle these challenges. *Matching this cognitive preference to the demands of the market place is crucial.* A singularly short term thinker cannot work out what conditions may be like in the future and will be unprepared. Likewise, a singularly focused long term thinker may miss current opportunities.

HOW BUSINESS IS CONDUCTED IN DIFFERENT CULTURES

The careers of previously successful North American executives can be found littered around different parts of the world. A North American working in Latin America fell on his sword when in the beginning of a negotiation he asks point blank: 'How do I know I won't get skewered on your local stock exchange?' This dealt a wicked blow to the proceedings when the Latin American counterparts muttered, 'This man doesn't even know us and he asks insulting questions like this!' In North America, the executive may have been admired for being forthright. Outside his country of origin, it spelled doom.

Personal Versus Contractual Business Relationships

In many studies executives demonstrated different culturally based competencies. To be successful in different cultures requires an ability both to understand and make choices on three basic continuums. The first is building business relationships. In many countries outside North America business relationships with strategic partners, suppliers, customers, government officials and others are built on the basis of personal relationships: ie, trust and mutual respect. The personal connection must precede the business arrangement which must often be done gradually. Managing face is another aspect of building personal relationships. Executives who do this show that they respect the position, the authority and age of their counterparts by appropriate manners, respecting symbols of office, by their speech and the way they demonstrate their own authority.

In contrast, the North American executive described above assumed that the way to build the relationship was contractual as he was used to in North America. The basis of our arrangement is that 'I have given you the best price, most closely meet your specifications and what you see is what you get.' In that context, the contractual nature of his question is evident. How can I be sure that I won't get hurt by this? And it is answered by specifying every aspect and bringing up even unpleasant questions. In the other cultural setting, 'How can I be sure that I won't get hurt by this' is answered by 'I know these people, they can be trusted, they won't hurt us.' Contracts are drawn in both situations, but what is more important is a critical cultural decision that an executive must make and implement.

Bias For Action: Where Do You Put Your Trust?

In deciding to act, what is the executive's biases? In some cultures, planning and spelling out contingencies is key to moving forward. In others the plan is secondary to who the person or people are who will implement the initiative. These differences can even appear between functions in the same organisation. The executive line management of a worldwide organisation was at odds with the leadership of the IT function. The bias for action of the line management was implementation not planning. 'I don't want to know the plan, just tell me what it will do and by the way, I have already told customers we will have it in six months.' The orientation of the IT function leadership is that 'I can't deliver anything of value without identifying your need, making the specifications, agreeing and deploying financial and personnel resources, establishing prototypes, testing and milestones. To do less will either lead to a product that may not meet your needs or a package that is constantly in need of repair, rework and patching over glitches.' The line management said, 'I expect you do all those things but I don't need to know them, just deliver it on time. You people are very hard to work with, you try to bureaucratise everything. If you don't deliver it on time, I am just going to outsource the whole function and find people who do what I ask without asking a lot of questions.'

Being able to operate at both ends of this spectrum of planning and implementation is crucial for the credibility and even the communication between parties. Often an executive thinks he/she is gaining credibility by explaining the plan of action when the cultural audience is only interested in when it will be implemented and by whom. Or they will tout the person who will lead the initiative and think that they will gain commitment, when the audience thinks the person is extraneous to success, that a well devised plan drives success and should be idiot-proof, that is, the success of the plan should be independent of the players.

Exercising Leadership: Push And Pull Strategies

Various cultures require a charismatic centralised authority where the leader is larger than life and is associated intimately with the vision of the organisation. Other cultures believe charisma to be anathema. The ability both to diagnose the situation in which each is appropriate and the ability to lead effectively in either a centralised or a participatory culture is essential to success today. Too many executives are unproductive because they are participatory when they need to be visionary and decisive. Others limit participation and so their vision remains their own because they cannot find any disciples. Knowing how and when and meeting current expectations is crucial.

Hay/McBer measures international adaptability by noting strengths in each of these factors. In the chart below, the strength of each component and the central tendency on the continuum as a whole is noted. The person depicted is strong on both personal and contractual relationships. On the basis for action the individual has less strength in implementation than in planning. For exercising authority he or she is more likely to exercise centralised, charismatic leadership than participatory leadership but show strength in both.

The graph on the following page points out the need for flexibility in today's executives. The likelihood that they will only need to do business in their own culture is fading, because technology will thrust many people together in a virtual mega-culture where previously they would not have interacted. So the ability to build business relationships differently, to rely on different basis for action and for gaining credibility and the need to exercise authority in various ways is crucial.

Executives do have more choices of where their personalities fit on the first two continuums, motivation and time horizon, because they can choose market places and organisations that reward with success the behaviours that naturally flow from their motives and cognitive styles. This choice is important because an executive's motivation and cognitive style is likely to remain stable over time, so the choice of situations or venues which support his or her natural characteristics is key. In the case of building relationships, basis

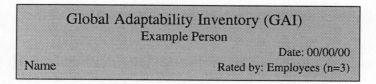

Global Adaptability Inventory (GAI)
Example Person

Name

Date: 00/00/00
Rated by: Employees (n=3)

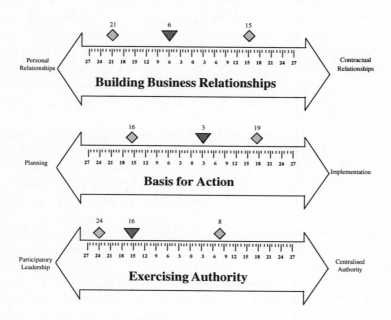

for action and exercising authority, although there may be natural tendencies to one end of the continuum or the other, executives can learn to be effective at both ends of the continuum.

Ponce DeLeon did not find the fountain of youth that would answer all his needs but he did discover Florida. Organisations cannot find the magic bullet that is available off the shelf to work in all situations but, with research and effort, they can augment the generic competencies that work across most situations with a set of unique competencies that will distinguish whether their success can be translated from one venue to another. In this way, as

McClelland has pointed out, combining the generic with the unique competencies enables the organisation to sort the successful from the typical executive not 50% of the time but rather 72% of the time. That is an excellent rate of success.

5

Developing the Leaders of Tomorrow at Unilever

Nick Boulter

Unilever – with operations in over 200 countries, 300,000 employees, revenues of over £25 billion pa and a world leader in brand management – is one of the world's most well-known companies, frequently rated by graduates as one of the best to work for anywhere.

It is also a company with a long tradition of training and development – with managers worldwide participating in internationally run training and management development programmes throughout key stages in their careers. It has also had for many years clear programmes for succession planning and career development that have established a global benchmark of best practice. Developing future management and leadership capability has always been a core concern.

During the 1980s and 1990s, in common with the other huge companies in its sectors – food, personal products, detergents and domestic chemicals – Unilever has faced the challenges of the market: de-regulation, the collapse of communism and the growth of the 'Asian tigers' opening up new markets, more knowledgeable and discriminating consumers, a stronger trade and the growth of own label products and the rapidity of change. Unilever has faced these challenges successfully through growing and internationalising its operations, focusing on the key categories and brands that will give greatest global returns, improving the innovation process and cutting costs.

Unilever knew that the capabilities of its managers were key to its success: capabilities not only at the top of the company but at all levels. In the early 1990s the company launched a widescale review of the effectiveness of its human resource policies – among which was whether the existing approaches for recognising and developing management potential were the best – not only for the company as it was then but as it would be in the foreseeable future. In particular it wanted to focus on the two areas of promotability and professionalism: promotability relating to the criteria and processes used in assessing the future potential of managers; and professionalism relating to the skills, knowledge and experience that managers must have in their professional areas — for instance finance, logistics etc.

DEVELOPING MANAGEMENT CAPABILITY

Unilever's executives adopted a total quality approach to the issue: they believed that you can only manage what you can measure. But they realised that the definitions they were using were no longer valid, and decided to launch into two major exercises – the purpose of which was to ensure:

- That Unilever worldwide had criteria and processes in place that enabled it to identify and select those top executives who had the potential to create the biggest successes or 'wins' for the business in the future.

- That Unilever managers worldwide were at the leading edge in their professional/ skill areas.

A Unilever project team, led by Dr David Jones, undertook a lot of benchmarking of other major companies to understand how they had approached these issues. With the assessment of potential it rapidly realised that a competency based approach was the way to go: that is to look at the behaviours that make a difference between acceptable and star performers, and to use such a framework to help identify the leaders of tomorrow. They also realised that they could put together a competency model that would be 75% all right fairly quickly, but wanted to ensure the framework really reflected Unilever's unique needs – and was not an imported generic model. Dr Jones' project team established some tough standards for the competency framework. It must:

- be acceptable to all levels of managers in all businesses;

- be linked to the future requirements of the business — not just those of the present, and certainly not to those of the past;

- be rooted in the behaviours of those managers who were already known to be successful in the developing business climate;

- be internationally applicable — across all Unilever's 200 or more territories;

- be easy to use by line managers and be non-bureaucratic.

The project team decided to work with outside consultants who could be global partners in this process, and who had a track record of success with other major companies. Hay/McBer was selected: the choice of Hay/McBer as global partner was made in the light of its track record with other major international companies.

A three stage process was put in place to achieve these objectives.

THE BEST AND THE VERY BEST

The starting point was an understanding of where the business was going, and for this lengthy interviews with each board director were conducted on a one-to-one basis. The issues covered were:

- What was the environment — markets, competition, regulatory etc — that executives would be operating in the future — as far out as could be seen?

- What would be the strategic challenges facing them?

- Who in the company at an executive level were seen to be operating in such environments and were seen to be examples of outstanding success?

- What was it that characterised these people?

Building on this the project team prepared a summary of the strategic issues facing the company and the strategic capabilities required by it. This was played back to the board members. Doing this was important for two reasons: it provided the business case against which a competency model could be tested and, if the strategic issues facing the company were to change, it would therefore provide a basis against which to assess the continuing relevance of the competency framework. After a number of reworkings these were agreed, and some of the key competencies likely to underpin success were hypothesised.

Unilever and Hay/McBer wanted the framework to be rooted on the behaviours and actions of people perceived as being outstanding performers in the organisation, and what these people actually thought, felt and did. This, longer term, would help in ensuring that a real behavioural shift to the standards of the very best could be developed. This was the second phase of the project – the identification of what the best actually do.

To get at this data a sample of senior executives were interviewed. The executives needed to be a good cross section of the senior executive population: some chairmen or other senior line people, some in senior functional roles; women and men; a balanced cross section by race, nationality and area of operation. In all 65 very senior managers were interviewed – two thirds of whom were 'superstars' (or the very best) and one third very good performers and stars in their own right (the best). They were all interviewed using a process known as behavioural event interviewing; this approach probes for the actions, thoughts and behaviours of the interviewee through the medium of significant events or situations, both successful and frustrating, which the interviewees had experienced in the recent past.

The interviews were taped, transcribed, coded by an expert analyst and used as part of a 'concept formation' process to understand the key competencies that characterised the really successful performers. In this the team involved were looking at the competencies that really differentiated the superstars from the stars – who were all effective performers; and what it was that particularly characterised outstanding success in Unilever. Using this a competency model was developed – 11 competencies were seen to differentiate the superior performers from the others. Some of these were similar to the competencies identified in the earlier interviews with the directors, but a number were new, and were ones that were unique to Unilever and not seen by the consultants in other high performing companies.

CULTURE FIT AND BUY-IN

Because of the high value Unilever places on consensus, gaining support or buy-in for the framework was critical, so the first process was to play the model back to the directors, other senior line managers and to senior personnel managers representative of the businesses internationally. Crucial here was to ensure that the language used was culturally neutral – that is, meant the same to a Dutch person as to an American, a French, a Japanese, an English person. This meant a lot of reworkings and redraftings, and finally the model was agreed – close to the research framework but with some language changes to embed it culturally in the organisation.

To ensure wider understanding and acceptance, senior Unilever managers ran workshops and made presentations: to chairmen, to senior personnel managers etc throughout the world.

The process by which the framework was to be implemented had to be non-bureaucratic, but nevertheless challenging: it had to provide a better basis for assessing the potential of future leaders than the previous processes. The solution was to build on the existing, clear, well managed processes but to incorporate an approach whereby company chairmen and other top line managers, when assessing a candidate, had to cite evidence that someone had demonstrated these competencies. No rules were placed on the requirement that a candidate must excel in so many competencies: simply that, in considering a candidate, evidence should be shown that the person already demonstrated these competencies. If the person did not demonstrate the competencies then the question was: is this person really ready for a more senior position? This process was piloted and a number of people who had previously deemed to be suitable for potential promotion were seen to fall short in some critical areas and vice versa. The assessors found that the competencies helped to probe deeper and therefore to be more rigorous in their selection. The intention was not only to stop unsuitable nominations, but also to ensure that those who previously, in the prevailing culture, might not have been deemed suitable, but who in fact had very high potential, were identified and did not leave the organisation in frustration. This broadening of the pool of talent for promotion was one of the benefits for the organisation in shifting to a more multinational culture.

OTHER APPLICATIONS

The competencies for the senior executives were formally adopted by the Unilever board in 1994, and now have been used successfully in two rounds of reviews. The exercise was seen as so valuable that it has also been cascaded down to the senior and middle management levels. For these levels the same competencies were used — but the descriptors varied by level. Each of these levels was derived from equally rigorous assessments of the competencies that differentiated success at the various levels.

PRACTICAL CREATIVITY	
Definition	*Creates new business insights which can be turned into new and realistic plans.*
Rationale	*In an increasingly competitive and rapidly changing world minor incremental change will not suffice. The ability to 'find new paths' is a business imperative.*
D	Identifies patterns or trends based on previous experience or established approaches, and combines elements to provide new and pragmatic solutions.
C	Understands and clarifies patterns, trends and underlying themes in information, both internal or external; understands the business implications and applications of these; generates innovative solutions to issues.
B	Integrates many ideas and observations about complex issues into clear concepts that create useful insights for the business – 'finds new paths'. Creates new insights from a wide range of information.
B+	Creates fresh and innovative concepts that are not obvious to others and that may be new for the company, or even the industry, and which may have a profound impact on the business. Finds ways, for example, to fully understand how consumers live and think in order innovatively to create new insights for the business. Is able to shift mind set.

An example of the competency, 'practical creativity' is shown above; in this, progression from 'D' to 'B+' represents increasing levels of seniority.

Since the introduction of the behavioural competencies — known as differentiating competencies — Unilever has also redefined the professional knowledge and skills needed by managers to be world class today. This has been for ten core professional areas and involved benchmarking best practice in other organisations as well as internal teams identifying the professional/skill needs for the future.

The differentiating competencies have become part of the vocabulary of Unilever managers now. The competency model is being applied into other areas — such as graduate recruitment and performance management — providing an underpinning and integrating framework for many human resources processes and applications.

The next major application now under way is for development: now the competencies are being used to select those with potential, how can they be used to help develop those managers not yet ready for promotion; and how can all managers improve on their weaker areas? To achieve this Unilever has launched a development process supported by 360 degree assessment – with the questions based around the competencies.

An audit of the application of the competencies is underway: this is testing user reactions, with the intention of introducing any desired modifications. This will ensure that the competencies remain valid and current and do not risk becoming ossified or set in stone. As job demands change so will aspects of the competencies and this ongoing research will ensure the renewed competencies will help deliver the very best performance.

Unilever is confident that the competencies and the management applications that draw on them, are making a big impact on their ability to perform better in the global economy.

6

Why do Outside Experienced Hires Fail? A Case Study of Competency-Based Assessment and Selection

Mary Fontaine

As corporations seek new ways to compete and win in global markets, one strategy they use more and more is to bring in executive talent from the outside. Companies look for people with the unique expertise and experience needed to enter new markets or create new products or services for important niches. Fewer and fewer corporations are relying exclusively on 'growing their own' executives. Buying talent and fresh perspective from the outside is on the rise.

There is a dilemma, however. While outside hires bring insight and expertise that would take too long to develop in-house (*if* it could be developed at all), these transplanted executives often fail. Failures are expensive — often well into six figures for the executive search fees alone.

This case study is about a corporation faced with this dilemma and how it is solving it. The company needs over 100 new executives each year to meet its worldwide growth objectives. Yet, the average tenure of executives hired in from the outside, in 1992, was just about three years. People who grew up inside and made it to the executive ranks had only a slightly better record, just over four years.

The company was (and is) aggressive in the market and extremely results-oriented. Its reputation has been one of chewing people up and spitting them out. Yet top level executives from other companies who were known to be aggressive and had significant market accomplishments in their careers could not make it here. This spelled significant cost and slow headway against the company's growth goals.

IDENTIFYING EXECUTIVES WHO WOULD SUCCEED

The challenge was twofold. The first part was identifying the characteristics of those executives who could lead the company's growth strategy and at the same time succeed in its unique culture. The second part was sourcing and then accurately identifying executives who possessed these capabilities. The company retained Hay/McBer as a partner in this effort.

To solve the first part of the problem, Hay/McBer consultants and a strong internal team from all the company's businesses conducted an executive leadership study. The first step was to identify, in light of the company's business strategy, the kinds of situations that future leaders would face and need to surmount to be successful. In a day long session, the company's chairman and the presidents of the businesses generated an agreed list of the most critical situations future leaders would need to master. They also indicated those situations current executives already handled well and those they did not.

The company was fortunate in already having a considerable number of executives who were good at the things that the top team identified would be critical for the future. The chairman and 50 of the most senior executives nominated 20 executives, out of the top 250+, who were the best examples of the kind of leadership needed to execute against the strategic situations. The project team of Hay/McBer and internal consultants then identified another sample of 20 solid and more typical executives, matched on sex, nationality, type of business, length of service and job level.

These 40 executives became the focus of intense study. Each participated in a three and a half hour Behavioural Event Interview and completed a full assessment battery, measuring their underlying motivation, level of optimism, leadership style and the climate they created. Their direct reports also completed surveys to describe how the executives led their teams and the impact they had. Hay/McBer compared the data from the outstanding group with that of the more typical group to identify the characteristics that led to success in strategic situations.

CULTURAL COMPETENCIES: COMPANIES WILL REJECT EXECUTIVES WHO AREN'T GOOD FITS

What emerged from the study was not what was expected. While the outstanding executives in this company were driven by constantly improving bottom-line results, they were not the ruthless, aggressive, 'churn and burn' group as reputed in the marketplace. In fact, as a group, the outstanding executives had incredibly positive respect for individuals, were very optimistic about what they and other people could achieve and were also motivated by forming strong personal relationships. Additionally, they were high in ego maturity and genuineness. In other words, they knew their own limitations and the limitations of others. They saw people issues in their full complexity and did not stereotype people or situations. As for genuineness, they were compelled to act consistently with what they thought and felt, so they could not lie – or even shade the truth.

After seeing what kind of people achieved outstanding results in this company, it became apparent that part of the reason for turnover with outside hires was because of a cultural mismatch. As explained by the top management team when they heard the results of the study, often executives who 'grew up' in very bureaucratic 'political' organisations did not fare well when they joined this company because they tried to 'manage the process and forgot about managing the business.' So executives who came in and tried to manage through position power, versus personal relationship building, or who withheld information to have power over others, were rejected, much like a body rejects a transplanted organ if the tissue is not a good match.

This finding changed the way the company recruited in two ways. Firstly, they were able to give search firms a much more detailed brief of the kind of executive who was a good fit to the organisation's culture. This led to sourcing from less traditional companies within and outside the industry.

Secondly, the company embarked on a more precise assessment process for executives they were considering hiring. CVs and traditional interviews were not good enough indicators of the characteristics that made executives a good or bad match to the organisation. Instead, the company began using the same kind of in-depth assessment (interviews and assessment batteries) for selection that was used in the initial study.

Using these cultural competencies as a screen has resulted in a much better 'hit rate' among executive hires. In the three years that this new selection process has been in place, turnover of executives hired through the process has been less than one-fifth the rate of turnover for executives hired outside the process.

Reviewing the competency studies of dozens of executive jobs conducted in the past three years we estimate that one to two-thirds of the competencies identified as distinguishing outstanding performers are culture — not job-related. In other words, they are characteristics that are required for the individual to fit in and be effective in the particular organisational culture, and not required per se for performing the job.

'COMPENSATORY MODELS' OF COMPETENCE: ONE SIZE DOESN'T FIT ALL

One thing became obvious in the original study of the company's executives: there were different kinds of outstanding leaders. Every person in the study was nominated against the twelve strategic situations to identify those which the executive was exemplary in handling. Based on these assessments, we could see that some executives were good at handling certain situations and other executives were good at handling others. Four groups emerged: general managers, turnaround leaders, people developers and strategic thinkers.

We then tested to see if there were differences in the competencies demonstrated by the different groups and there were. For example, the strategic thinkers were stronger conceptually than other executives. The turnaround leaders and people developers were higher in the socialised power motive. This confirmed that there were different ways to be successful in the company.

We had the opportunity two years later to validate the original model against a larger sample of 72 senior executives. Most of the original competencies continued to differentiate outstanding versus more typical performance. (This time the criteria for performance was 'performance against annual operating plan' as measured by part of the executive's bonus payout.) More importantly, we had enough data to work out which different combinations of the competencies predicted outstanding performance.

Instead of having a fixed list of competencies which everyone is supposed to possess to be outstanding, David McClelland, McBer's founder and chairman, was able to create an algorithm that allowed the possession of one competency to compensate for the absence of another competency. In this algorithm, he found that one out of three 'personal initiative' competencies, plus one out of three 'organisational influence' competencies, plus four other competencies (primarily the 'cultural competencies') was an excellent predictor of performance. In fact, this flexible 'compensatory' competency algorithm was so robust that it accurately predicted who would get outstanding performance 74% – 86% of the time in three new executive populations (two of whom were Europeans and Asians).

The following two tables show the predictive nature of the compensatory algorithm. Table 6.1 shows the compensatory algorithm applied to 29 of the executives assessed in 1992 as part of the original study and who received bonuses for performance against their 1993 annual operating plan. This table also shows the algorithm applied against a totally new sample of 43 executives who were assessed during 1992–1993 who received bonuses for their performance against their 1993 annual operating plan. The table shows the percentage of executives who were assessed by the algorithm as outstanding (ie, they possessed one of the three personal initiative competencies, one of the three organisational effectiveness competencies and at least four other leadership competencies) and also received in the top third of the bonus payouts, which was considered outstanding bonus performance by the company.

Table 6.1 Predicting top bonus performance from compensatory competency algorithm

Classified by compensatory algorithm as:	Initial sample of executives n=29		New sample of executives n=43	
	Number	% receiving bonus in top 1/3 of 1993 bonus pool	Number	% receiving bonus in top 1/3 of 1993 bonus pool
Highly qualified	12	100% (n=12)	17	65% (n=11)
Less qualified	17	24% (n=4)	26	19% (n=5)
Measure of association*		.93**		.66**
Percent correctly predicted	25/29	86%	32/43	74%

* based on Tetrachoric R: this measures the association between being highly qualified and receiving a bonus in the upper one third of payments
** p<0.01

Table 6.2 shows the compensatory algorithm applied to two new samples, one of European executives working in Europe and one of Asian executives working in Asia at the time of the assessment and bonus payout. The algorithm was essentially the same for the European and Asian sample, the only differences being that (a) some of the specific competencies were different[1] and (b) demonstration of a total of seven, not six, competencies was needed to be classified as outstanding. There was no bonus data on these two groups, so nominations from the company's top executives were used to define which executives were outstanding performers. Like Table 6.1, Table 6.2 shows the percentage and number of executives who were classified by the compensatory algorithm as highly qualified or less qualified who were nominated as outstanding.

---

[1] The original leadership model was cross validated in Europe and Asia. Some of the original leadership competencies did not work in other national cultures, eg, optimism did not predict outstanding performance in Asia, and some new competences did predict performance (eg, balancing demands between headquarters and local markets predicted outstanding performance in Europe and Asia).

Table 6.2 Predicting outstanding performance among other nationalities from compensatory competency algorithm

	European executives n=19		Asian executives n=16	
Classified by compensatory algorithm as:	Number	% who were nominated as outstanding performers	Number	% who were nominated as outstanding performers
Highly qualified	11	82% (n=9)	7	86% (n=6)
Less qualified	8	13% (n=1)	9	11% (n=1)
Tetrachoric R measure of association	(pooled because of the small sample sizes) .90**			
Percent correctly predicted	(also pooled because of the small samples sizes) 30/35 or 86%			

** $p < 0.01$

CONCLUSION

By paying attention to the unique culture of the company and by applying a more flexible set of competency criteria, this company has been able to solve the problem of the need to bring in outside executives and not have them rejected by the organisation. The experience with this company has provided groundbreaking insight in how to get the most robust use of executive competency models in executive selection. They are also making advances in using the competencies for advice to help new executives under-stand cultural as well as job requirements. The aim here is to increase even more the chance that new executives will succeed. It seems to be working. New executive hires who received advice from their assessment against the competencies performed 10% better than executives who were assessed but who did not receive any advice.

Organisations need to pay attention to what is unique about their organisational requirements for leaders. Some of the competency requirements are to do with the nature of the challenges that the leader will face at that point in time in the organisation's life. Some of the requirements have more to do with the culture of the organisation and what behaviour it will accept and not reject in its executives. The latter often is the bigger determinant of whether the executive will succeed and be worth the investment in an outside search.

7

Managing for Motivation and Performance Improvement

Jim Burruss

At the age of 32, John Jones[1] had ten years of experience with Mobil Oil. He had joined the company shortly after graduating with an engineering degree from a small, mid-western American university. John Jones went to work in one of Mobil's older refineries. He progressed quickly in his first five years and spent his past five years as director of operations in three different refineries.

John Jones had just completed a five-day, company-sponsored management development programme. There, he learned about the concept of organisational climate and its relationship to performance. During the programme several of his peers enquired why he had rated his organisation as high on 'standards' while they had rated *their* organisations as only moderate.

John Jones reflected for a moment and explained that, 'Over the past five years, I have spent a lot of time at five of our refineries and actually worked at the same job in three of them. It seems to me that, at any other refinery in our system, I would have the same job title but the work I'd be doing would be two levels below what I'm doing here. *I bet I've learned more in the one year that I've been here than I did in the entire four years I spent in the other two refineries.'*

---

[1] John Jones is a pseudonym for a participant JAB had in a Mobil MMPI in Beaumont, TX in the mid-1980s.

These sentiments are characteristic of people who have had the benefit of working in an environment that promotes professional development. They report that they are energised by the experience. They are clearly challenged by it. They seem to acknowledge the learning that has occurred but, most of all, they appreciate the fact that they are performing at a much higher level than they ever did before.

Such environments seem to tap into a reservoir of motivation that most organisations miss. This reservoir is what we refer to as **discretionary effort**. It is the level and quality of effort that people have to give over and above that which is necessary to keep their job. We have also observed that, the more complex the job, the more discretionary effort is available to the person in that job.

HOW TO DO IT

We learned about individual competencies by studying what the outstanding performers do that distinguishes them from typical performers. We used a similar strategy to work out why some organisations are much better than others at creating environments where people can best develop their competencies.

What we have found is that:

1. there are not a lot of organisations or managers that do this very well;

2. those that do are diligent and purposeful in their efforts and;

3. their efforts usually result in measurable performance improvements, for both the individual and the organisation, in about 70% of the cases.

THE CURRENT NORMS IN ORGANISATIONS

While most managers see themselves as coaching and developing their direct reports, few are actually effective at it. The overwhelming majority of today's workers report that they are constantly scrambling to keep up with the volume of work and the rapid changes that are taking place in their industry. At the same time they protest that their organisation is not making the best use of their capabilities. They see themselves as being somewhat overwhelmed by the amount of work but under-appreciated and underused in the quality of their contributions.

One revealing study by Yankelovich, Skelly, and White (YSW)[2] noted that only 28% of the workforce reported that they were, 'Giving as much as I can possibly give to my job.' In contrast, 76% of their respondents said that they, 'Would be willing to give more to the organisation if it were better managed.' The difference between those two responses symbolises the untapped potential available.

Apparently, whatever it is that managers feel they are doing to coach and develop their employees, it is not being perceived as motivating by their direct reports. To understand why, it is necessary to take a closer look at the key components of an effective development process.

MOTIVATION AND JOB REQUIREMENTS

The simplistic view that all you need is money to keep people motivated, ignores the complexity of individuals and shackles organisations with an insatiable demand for escalating pay. True, if you want high performance, you must be willing to pay for it. However, most managers have learned from experience that willingness to pay for high performance is no assurance that you will get it.

Psychologists define motives as natural energisers. Motives are not something outside the person, nor can they be given to someone. Rather, like any biological drive, motives are deep-seated characteristics of the individual. Motives are indicative of how a person thinks about situations. They reflect what he or she finds intrinsically satisfying, naturally enjoys, would be inclined to do even if they were not getting a paycheck for it.

---

[2] *Values in the Work Place*, Yankelovich, Skelly, and White, 1985.

People and Competencies

Like other competencies, motives predict how someone will react and perform in a given role. People who are particularly high on the achievement motive, for example, seem to be constantly searching for ways to test themselves in their environment. They set challenging goals for themselves and are motivated by the clear sense of mastery against those targets. Such individuals tend to thrive in environments where there are:

1. clear standards of excellence;

2. personal responsibility for the outcome;

3. immediate, concrete feedback from a credible source.

People who are high in the socialised power motive, on the other hand, are not concerned about individual mastery. They focus on the impact or influence that certain behaviours or events have on others. Their enjoyment comes from situations that provide them with the opportunity to have a desired effect on others.

The affiliation motive concentrates people on the establishment and maintenance of close friendly relationships. People who are high on this motive are energised by the opportunities to engage with people that they like. Those interactions need not have any purpose other than the relationship itself.

While all of us must have substantial levels of all three motives just to survive, what distinguishes individuals is the unique combination of these motives that we bring to a given situation. Successful entrepreneurs, for example, tend to be high on the achievement motive, low on affiliation, and low-moderate on power. Most effective CEOs tend to be low-moderate on achievement, low on affiliation, and high on socialised power. Effective mid-level managers in matrixed organisations are typically moderate in all three and, we have found outstanding turnaround leaders to be high on both achievement and socialised power and relatively low on affiliation.

These combinations are practically endless, however, they do illustrate the value of matching people well to jobs in the first place. An effective developmental plan should start by assessing the match between the job requirements and the person's motive disposition.

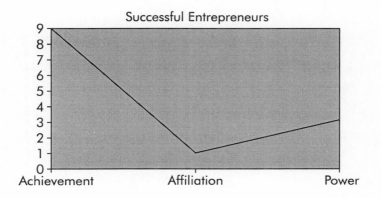

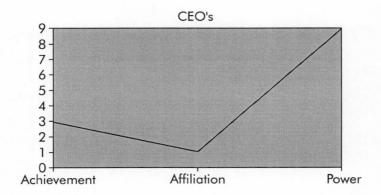

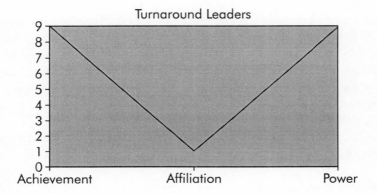

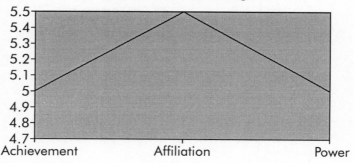

Understanding motivation helps us to look at competency development from several important standpoints. They help us to:

- Appreciate the fact that people are motivated differently;

- Understand why individuals respond differently in similar situations;

- Determine what conditions arouse particular motives in ourselves and others;

- Monitor and manage our own motives to be more effective managers.

MANAGERIAL STYLES AND PRACTICES

If managers are going to be effective at coaching and developing their direct reports, they need first to understand their own motivation. For example, it is common for managers to have risen to positions of leadership because of their own achievement motive.[3] They have set high standards for themselves, taken personal responsibility for their performance, and used whatever feedback was available to help themselves improve.

As managers, however, that same orientation can become a major obstacle to coaching and developing others. Instead of focus-

---

[3] AT&T study: McClelland and Boyatzis, 1982 [*Human Motivation*, p. 253, 1985]

ing on the developmental needs of their direct reports, these managers continue to concentrate on their own performance and mastery. They are motivated not by the opportunity for challenging and developing others but, rather, for the sense of gratification that they get from being able to solve a difficult problem when others cannot.

The fact that motives operate at the subconscious and intuitive level makes the situation all the more difficult to manage. It is as if they have been programmemed to repeat the successes of their past and they lose sight of the impact they are having on others. This managerial style is what we refer to as pacesetting.

By contrast, managers who are high on the coaching style take a quite different approach. They are at least as concerned about the long-term development of the individual they are working with as they are about solving the immediate problem. Consequently, they are much more inclined to help that person learn how to think about such situations rather than just making suggestions or quizzing the person as to whether they know the right answer.

Coaching managers tend to be operating out of the socialised power motive.[4] They are supportive and encouraging but they are not uncomfortable with being confrontational. They are constantly looking for opportunities to help others reach their full potential. As a result of this influence, others usually feel stronger and more capable of doing what they feel they should be doing.

A high affiliation motive often inclines a manager to use the affiliative managerial style. This focuses the manager's efforts on maintaining good relationships with specific individuals in the organisation. Managers try to cultivate harmony by avoiding conflict in the organisation. They are supportive and encouraging but have a difficult time confronting performance problems objectively.

Similar relationships can be seen between the three social motives and the coercive, authoritative, and democratic managerial styles. Just as each individual has a unique combination of motives, each manager has a unique combination of managerial styles.

---

[4] McClelland, David C, 'Power and Organisational Leadership', Chapter 6 from *Power: The Inner Experience*, 1975.

THE RELATIONSHIP BETWEEN MOTIVES AND MANAGERIAL STYLES			
Manager's dominant motive	Situational pressure	Managerial style	Motive aroused in employee
Achievement	Low	Pacesetting	Achievement or power
	High	Coercive	Power
Affiliation	Low	Affiliation	Affiliation
	High	Democratic	The dominant motive of the person
Personal Power	Low	Authoritative	Power or achievement
	High	Coercive	Power
Socialised Power	Low	Coaching	The dominant motive of the person
	High	Authoritative	Power or achievement

The figure above oversimplifies the situational variables involved in this process to highlight the relationship between each motive and style. In fact, the combination of styles that a manager uses at a particular time is a function of many different things. It is influenced by the nature of the task and the competencies of the person responsible for that task. It is influenced by the cultural norms and prevalent practices within the organisation. It is influenced by the skill and experience that the manager brings to the situation. However, across all these, it is influenced most consistently by the motives and values that individual managers bring to the workplace.

Few managers, then, are naturally inclined to be effective at coaching and developing others. Most have to work consciously at it. They must work at balancing *other influences in the environment* that would work against the development of others. They must also manage the motives and values within themselves that interfere with effective coaching. Specifically, they must manage their own achievement and affiliation arousal and cultivate more of the socialised power motive.

ORGANISATIONAL CLIMATE: STANDARDS, RESPONSIBILITY AND REWARDS

The final component of an effective developmental process is the organisational climate. We define climate as employees' perceptions of those aspects of the environment that directly affect their ability to do their jobs well. When the climate is positive, people are motivated and excited about what they are doing. When it is negative, people are relatively depressed and angry. It is no surprise, then, that organisational climate is an excellent predictor of organisational performance.

Of the six dimensions that make up organisational climate, three have particular relevance to professional development. Standards refers to the emphasis the organisation places on excellence. It is a measure of the extent that everyone is pushed to do their best. One of the best indicators of high standards is the prevalence of challenging but attainable goals. This applies to the organisation as well as to the individuals within that organisation.

Organisations that excel at developing their people are also very high on responsibility. Individuals feel that they have the freedom to do their jobs as they would like but that they are also accountable for the outcome. One of the most important aspects of this is the feeling that they are encouraged to use their discretionary judgement. When faced with situations where the conventional wisdom does not fit their view of what would be best for the situation, employees feel encouraged to use their own best judgement.

Such organisations are also high on the rewards dimension. Individuals feel that they are provided with valuable performance feedback. Specifically, they know what it is their manager and/or the organisation values in their contributions. They also know specifically what the organisation would like to see more or less of from them. They know where they stand. They know specifically what it is that they need to do to repeat their successes as well as what they need to do to deal with their shortcomings.

Employees' perceptions of these dimensions of climate are influenced by many variables. For example, professional service employees often feel that responsibility is even more important than rewards. Even within the same industry, an individual's perception of standards is highly influenced by that person's previous experience and training. Business volatility, geographic proximity, organisational structure, and level within the organisation are only a few of the many variables that affect the climate.

Still, managerial practices consistently emerges as the most important single variable affecting organisational climate. Most employees already know intuitively that, if you want to change the climate quickly, you need to change the management. Fairly sophisticated path analysis studies by social science researchers seem to confirm that view.[5]

PUTTING IT ALL TOGETHER

The three dimensions of climate that promote competency development are similar to the conditions necessary to arouse and sustain the achievement motive. These are the dimensions that are most directly affected by the coaching managerial style. From a causal standpoint, the coaching managerial style leads to high standards, responsibility and rewards, which arouse the achievement motive and competency development in others. However, managers who are most effective at using the coaching style are driven by the socialised power motive.

Competency development then, is not so much a complicated process as it is a diligent, thoughtful one. To exhibit effective coaching behaviours, managers need to monitor and manage their own motivations. This requires a certain amount of self-awareness about their motives and related competencies.

Managers also need to have some appreciation for the natural motivation that individuals bring to their jobs. By paying more

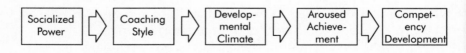

---

[5] ISSR Studies @ University of Michigan, 1985

attention to these internal energisers, managers are better able to match people to jobs. For example, if you place a person who is low in the power motive in a job that requires a lot of directing and influencing others, it could either enhance their development or curtail their career. The difference is the level of support and coaching available to them.

Finally, managers can be much more effective at competency development if they recognise the many leverage points they have for creating a positive climate for change. The standards dimension, for example, can be influenced by the goal-setting process, the quality of dialogue about expectations and performance, and modelling. The responsibility dimension can be influenced by job design, organisational structure, and role clarification. The rewards dimension can be influenced by development discussions, praise and recognition, and compensation. Managers have a lot more options and responsibility, than simply sending the employee to a training programme.

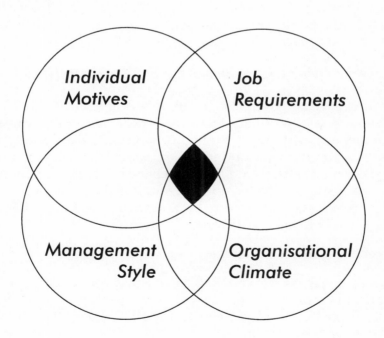

SUMMARY AND RECOMMENDATIONS

With these principles in mind, the competency development process involves six major steps.

1. Recognition of the competency

The first step in developing a particular competency is recognising it when we see it and appreciating its contribution to excellent performance. Employees need to have opportunities to be educated about the competencies that are particularly important to their development.

2. Understanding the competency

The next step is understanding the types of situations that require that competency. At this stage it is most helpful to examine situations in which the competency was present as compared to those in which it was absent. This kind of exercise helps the person to internalise the competency enough to know when it is missing.

3. Experimenting with demonstration of the competency

A particularly important stage in the competency acquisition process is the opportunity to try new behaviours. This involves experimenting with ways of thinking and acting that are different from those used previously, and/or expanding the range of thinking and acting related to the competency. It is most important at this stage for the individual to have access to the advice and counsel that is necessary to make accurate assessments of his or her performance and to make corrective adjustments.

5. Practising using the competency

This step involves practice, using the competency in a variety of situations. The reputation in using the competency ensures that it becomes as natural and available as any other capability the person has previously demonstrated.

6. Applying the competency in job situations and in the context of other characteristics

Finally, the individual must integrate the competency with other competencies, thoughts, and behaviours in real job situations. This usually requires much practice as the individual develops greater appreciation and sophistication with the targeted competency.

8

Coaching in – Appraisal out

Frank Hartle

Is there anything new to be said about performance management? Surely it has all been said before?

In many organisations performance management remains as a relic from the past. It is still being run as a once a year event only; using the same old forms and seemingly focusing employees on objectives that are remote from the real needs of the business. However, in some organisations — an ever growing number — new forms of performance management are emerging. These new models are more powerful and are making a more significant contribution to business results. At the heart of these new models is the use of competencies as a tool to provide a common language to define, assess and develop individual performance throughout the organisation.

Looking at performance management in many organisations we can see five models of performance management (see Figure 8.1).

Model 1 is the familiar annual appraisal – the once a year event, often referred to unflatteringly, as the annual ritual. This can be of some limited value but it is commonly regarded as a low value process. 'We go through the motions but nothing seems to be different after the appraisal.'

Model 2 is performance management which is designed to be a continuous process throughout the business cycle. Objectives are

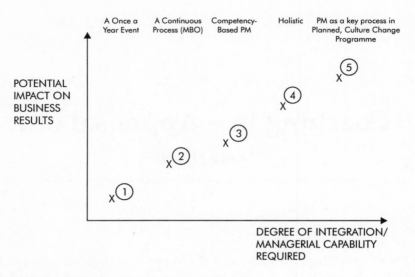

Figure 8.1 Models of Performance Management

set, performance is monitored throughout the year and performance reviews are carried out at the end of the cycle. This model started to appear in the 1980s when many organisations became more performance orientated. There was an increased focus on defining the outputs of jobs and on linking job objectives to the strategic objectives of the organisation. This was the era of management by objectives. As a result, performance management began to grow out of its appraisal box as planning for performance gained ground. Unfortunately many organisations have not moved beyond this level, they haven't opened the box that's protecting the old performance management process and dusted it off, although many other aspects of their structure and management processes might have changed significantly.

Models 3, 4 and 5 have emerged in the last five years, mainly as a reflection of the changing shape of organisations and the emergence of certain management styles. The culture of successful organisations in the 1990s is characterised more by empowerment than command and control, by devolution rather than hierarchy central control, and by ever increasing emphasis on serving and delivering customer needs (both external and internal customers). These organisations realise that performance improvement will be achieved only through a continuous learning/coaching culture in which self-management plays an increasingly important part. This work climate requires new ways of managing performance and a performance management process which is closely integrated to the business needs and cultural characteristics of the organisation.

Model 3 is a performance management process which incorporates competencies. This is known as the mixed model because through this process each individual is made aware of *what* results have to be achieved and *how* they will be achieved. Competencies provide the language to define the desired behaviours which enable performance achievement and improvement. Sometimes they will define the 'dimensions' of personal development that apply to everyone in the organisation. In some organisations eg Unilever, the Anglo Dutch consumer goods giant, the competencies define the 'breakthrough' behaviours which characterise the top performers. Clearly this behavioural model can be used in a number of other HR processes, such as recruitment, selection, succession planning and development. By providing staff with a clear vision of *what* has to be achieved and a precise language to define *how* the results will be achieved, competency-based performance management is a powerful process to bring about both short- and long-term performance improvement. Many organisations have adopted this model.

Model 4 is where the competency-based performance management process is closely integrated with other key processes within the organisation. For example, in ICI Fertilisers the process is closely integrated with business planning so that there is a closer alignment between corporate, team and individual objectives. This ensures that everyone has common business/job aims. Also this company has defined a set of core values and these are incorporated in the performance management process as a set of essential behaviours for all staff. These core values are defined as:

- team leadership;

- achievement focus;

- customer focus;

- concern for quality;

- developing others;

- influencing others.

In other organisations, the performance management process is linked with total quality or other related initiatives. In the UK many organisations are realising the value of linking Investors in People with the performance management process. They are complementary processes.

Model 5 is where competency-based performance management is used as a key process to bring about and reinforce *planned* culture change. By using competency models to define the desired behaviours in the new culture, and incorporating them into the performance management process, the organisation is able to create a powerful vehicle for driving and reinforcing culture (ie, behaviour) change, working alongside other HR processes such as Reward, Development and Work Definition.

Our proposition is that the further performance management progresses beyond models 1 and 2, the greater its potential impact on business results. The incorporation of competencies into performance management in models 3, 4 and 5 ensures that both the 'what' and the 'how' of performance are defined and assessed. This gives performance management the power to change behaviours, through focused development, and hence to improve performance, both short and long term. But as the models become more forward looking, developmental and integrated with other processes, the higher the level of managerial capability required to manage performance effectively. This has implications for the management training required in any development of existing performance management processes beyond models 1 and 2.

THE MIXED MODEL APPROACH

When we talk to people about performance management we often hear: 'we have figured out how to measure outcomes, but we're still struggling to recognise and reward the behaviour that leads to those outcomes'. Now many organisations are trying to identify and track performance using a variety of measures such as quality, customer satisfaction, leadership and teamworking. These measures are more human-sounding than profits and losses but they are still big concepts that are hard for people to understand. Without a performance management process that is aligned to this 'balanced scorecard' approach, companies will have a difficult time matching individual performance with the new set of measures. Competencies can be the key to translating non-financial goals into fair and appropriate standards of behaviour. They provide the level of detail organisations need to define 'the big picture' version of performance on a human scale. By giving each job holder a picture of the behaviours required for superior performance, the organisation is producing a powerful process for self-improvement.

The integration of competencies into the performance management process allows organisations to define performance both in terms of short term objectives and the long term development required in each job holder. But it is essential that both manager and job holder understand what the competencies are and how they should be used in the performance management process.

Example : John, a computer systems designer

The importance of having a competency framework to describe the performance expectations in a job and to assess individual performance achievement is illustrated in the story of John, a computer systems designer in a Dutch software company.

John joined the company at the age of 25. He was regarded as a graduate with high potential. From the start he was one of

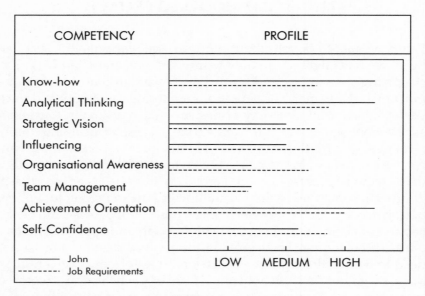

Figure 8.2 John versus job requirements in first job

the best systems designers in the team. Figure 8.2 shows John's score on the company selection questionnaire in combination with the job requirements.

This example shows that John fitted in well with the job competency requirements. His know-how, ability to think in an analytical way and his strong competitive spirit (achievement orientation) made him suitable. Although he lacked a few other aspects, eg organisational awareness, and influencing it is no surprise that he performed excellently in his first job.

His career proceeded excellently. He took on larger projects and handled them successfully. He was being stretched and he coped well. After a few successful years he was promoted to the job of technical manager – a manager of managers.

In the early days in this role all seemed well, but after a time he started to lose his grip on the job. People made important decisions without consulting him. Others complained that

John should concentrate on the broad outlines of policy and not on-line details of projects. His promotion began to look like a mistake. But how could this have happened? His start had been most promising and he had held several managerial posts with great success. Why was he failing now? Figure 8.3 shows John's profile in comparison with the requirements for the technical manager's job.

In comparison with his previous jobs, his new role required a much greater independent development of vision, and the ability to convince people, to gain their commitment to his vision – strong team leadership qualities and the ability to recognise and persuade the key players in the organisation. This job did not really challenge his expertise and mental acuteness. What John did, however, was to concentrate too much on the technical content of projects and too little on managing the business/ organisational environment, both in a strategic and managerial sense He continued to be a technical expert. As a result, he left people alone until

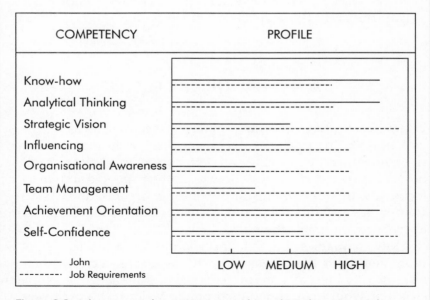

Figure 8.3 John versus job requirements in his technical manager job

the problems cropped up. Then he would jump in and fix the problem himself. People who reported to him became frustrated. They lacked clear direction and communication and felt John should spend more time helping them develop. As a result of this behaviour his isolation increased and he could not exert any real influence to provide resources or promotions and pay rises for his people. Hence they felt unrecognised and unsupported. John became frustrated. Eventually, he burned out.

This is a clear case of insufficient use of talent – something that might have been avoided if John's company had a more effective performance management process in place. An early diagnosis of the match between John's demonstrated competencies and the new job's requirements would have revealed the need for remedial action. John's manager could have worked with him to build stronger visionary, team leadership and influencing qualities. An even earlier diagnosis would have revealed that John was unlikely to be fit for a managerial job without prior development of certain competencies. Unfortunately, these details never surfaced.

A MODEL FOR THE FUTURE

Competencies have become popular in recent years as businesses look beyond financial indicators to measure performance. Mergers, re-engineering, downsizing and flatter structures have forced businesses to take a closer look at how to motivate people and turn their focus towards redefining and realising organisational strategy. Companies are embracing competencies as a way to put values into operations and make them real.

How companies choose to incorporate competencies varies. For example Praxair, the US gas company, assembled a cross-functional task force to identify core professional and managerial competencies that would support the corporate vision. All employees are now asked to focus on the same set of behaviours.

A major UK chemicals company has incorporated an 'essential behaviours' checklist into its performance management process. The essential behaviours describe the number of elements which the company sees as important in the process of achieving objectives. 'It's not just what you do that counts, it's how you do it.'
The behaviours are:

- teamwork and flexibility;

- innovation;

- initiative;

- customer service;

- working standards;

- communication;

- team leadership.

Job holders are assessed on the degree to which they regularly display these behaviours. Each behaviour is given a percentage weighting to indicate its importance to the role and the behaviours constitute 30% of the total appraisal 'score'. The appraisal score — a combination of the achievement of objectives (70%) and the display of behaviours (30%) — is linked directly to pay.

What is particularly interesting in this scheme is the attempt to position objective setting and essential behaviours within a balanced scorecard framework. The company has set key performance targets, incorporating such measures as return on capital, cash generation and upper quartile performance (against competitors). It has developed a set of fifteen 'integrated performance measures' to track company performance and help drive it towards these targets. The measures include not only factors like margins and plant reliability but also customer satisfaction and employee morale and motivation. Each business unit and manufacturing location uses its own related performance measures to identify and track its contribution to meeting the company's performance targets, through the performance management process. This integrated performance model is set out in Figure 8.4.

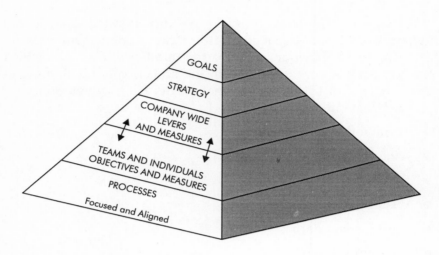

Figure 8.4 Integrated Performance Model

Other companies give more latitude to individuals, teams and business groups to select competencies that meet their needs. Rather than using competencies to drive a single corporate culture, these companies tailor them at the team and individual level.

WHEN IS IT WORTHWHILE?

Building a set of competency models can be expensive and laborious but it is worthwhile because it gives empirical evidence of behaviours that occur more often among superior performers. Before starting, it may be helpful to look at the situations where competency based performance management processes are particularly appropriate:

● **Uncertain environments** By now, most of us have heard stories about executives who praise their teams, even when they fail to meet financial targets. These people recognise that no one can win against the all powerful market place. In rapidly changing environments, where results are not under employee control, hard results objectives are often rendered irrelevant by external events. In such situations, assessment of performance must be based on whether employees did everything they could, whether they demonstrated the right behaviours – which would have led to successful achievements in other circumstances. The less control employees have over results, the more their performance should be based on demonstration of critical competencies.

● **Qualitative/process service jobs** In jobs with no relevant measurable outcomes – qualitative skills – competencies – are the best indication of employee performance, eg, for general assistants in supermarket chains – competency behaviours – such as being friendly and helpful to irritable customers, being well organised and tidy minded, anticipating customer enquiries – are the job requirements. The more subjective the job output, the more important it is to use competencies as the basis for the performance management process.

● **Self-managed teams** In teams, individual results outputs may be less important than their contribution to the group process. Team work/leadership competencies are increasingly important in organisations. The more important team performance is, as opposed to individual performance, the more important it is to appraise the teamwork behaviours of individual employees.

● **Developmental jobs** Where particular jobs are designed to grow. The more a job stresses the development of skills, e.g. management trainee positions, the more appraisal should be based upon demonstration of competencies.

● **Changing organisations** In changing organisations, employees' potential to contribute to the organisation in the future may be more important than their past performance. Most performance management systems are past oriented. The greater the emphasis on future performance, the more the performance management process should use the competency framework to stress the development and appraisal of competencies.

THE LINK WITH PAY

Results: that is what all this leads up to. But how do you pay for them? For most companies, pay is seen as a celebration of a change in attitude and behaviour – the icing on the cake. But they are right in holding back before making a leap. Keeping the performance management process separate from pay establishes the new dynamic – the way of doing things in the organisation – without the pressure and confusion that always accompanies pay. It enables a focus on performance improvement, not rewarding past standards or results. But employees will expect to be rewarded for their achievements. In Chapter 9, we will explore the connection between competencies and pay.

REFERENCES

Hartle, F (1995) *How to Re-engineer the Performance Management Process*, Kogan Page (UK).

Hartle, F Weiss, T Armstrong, S (1996) *How to Re-engineer the Performance Management Process* (US Version). Kogan Page/American Society of Training and Development.

9

Relating Pay to Competencies

Derek Pritchard

WHY RELATE PAY TO COMPETENCIES?

From the 1950s until fairly recently, the management of pay has been dominated by the notion of the job. People in most organisations have been paid largely according to their job: internal pay relativities have been driven by assessment of job size through some kind of job evaluation process; and external pay market comparisons have been made on a job basis, either by comparing pay rates directly with similar jobs outside or by using evaluated job size based comparisons.

In its simplest form – rate for the job – no account is taken of the performance or capability of the *person* in the job, except that the person must satisfy the requirements of the job to remain in it. The only way to reward high performance or capability is to promote the individual to a bigger, more demanding job.

While this simple rate-for-the-job approach persists in some areas, particularly for some manual employees, most businesses have made attempts over the years to take some account of the individual, especially for managerial, professional, technical and clerical work. In some areas, this has led to incremental pay progression, rewarding time spent in the job – either to reward 'loyalty', or based on the rather questionable assumption that capability and performance grow consistently with time.

More direct attempts to relate pay progression to individual performance have led to widespread use of pay ranges for each job (or grade of jobs), with movement through the range driven by some form of performance appraisal. But here again, until recently, the focus of the appraisal was typically based heavily on the achievement of hard, quantifiable objectives, derived from the basic accountabilities of the job.

This job-focused view of pay was entirely consistent with the organisational principles adopted by most companies during that period. Organisations were largely designed around clear structures and hierarchies, with great concentration on clarity and stability of roles, and in which the basic unit of work was 'the job'.

What has changed in recent years, and what has led to the growing interest in relating pay to competencies, is the progressive challenging of this structuralist view of organisation. Most organisations are changing – not just changing their structures, cutting a bit off here, and tacking a bit on there – but much more fundamentally the way in which they are organised.

Delayering; team working; project working; flexibility; organising around businesses processes; lateral rather than vertical career development — these are all areas of change for most organisations in today's environment. Together, they challenge the notion of a job defined purely in structural/hierarchical terms, and hence the pay management processes which have been built up on this model. In particular, they challenge the traditional separation of 'jobs' and 'people', and the way that these issues have been handled through separate management processes.

In a more flexible environment, roles can be shaped by the people in them. Take, for example, the growing use of multi-functional teams in customer service. The members of that team share the same common purpose – to provide high quality service to customers, answer queries effectively and so on. But the level at which each individual team member can actually contribute to this common purpose will be heavily influenced by his or her personal capability, in terms of skills and competencies. It seems entirely reasonable that the pay of the individual should in some way reflect the skills and competencies which they bring and use, and so encourage the development of these skills and competencies.

When these organisational changes began to gather speed in the mid-to-late 1980s, the reaction from some commentators was an extreme one. 'Let's base pay **entirely** on skills and competencies', they suggested. 'Let's abandon the idea of jobs altogether, and all the inflexible, rigid pay structures based on job evaluation, which go with it.' Like most pendulum-swing reactions, these suggestions have not been borne out in practice. There are very few examples of pay structures based entirely on competencies, and those organisations which attempted it have since found the need to build back in some consideration of job, or role in balance with the 'people' perspective of competencies.

The reasons for this are threefold:

1. In most organisations, people do not work in a totally unstructured environment, where what they do is only determined by their capability. Most work within defined roles, which place certain requirements and limitations on what they can do and hence the range of capability which they need – although the **degree** of flexibility of role may be much greater than in the past.

2. Relating pay only to competencies, without regard for output or contribution can risk generating a culture concentrating only on inputs, at variance with the ever-increasing demands for business performance and achievement.

3. Similarly, it may result in paying for competencies which are not actually used or needed, and hence escalation of pay costs without any equivalent business benefit.

It is now much more widely recognised that paying only for competencies is just as one-sided a view as paying only for jobs. The more recent ventures into relating pay to competencies have taken a more balanced perspective in which it is recognised that pay needs to be related to a number of factors, including:

- the role;
- the skills and competencies of the individual;
- the performance and results achieved;

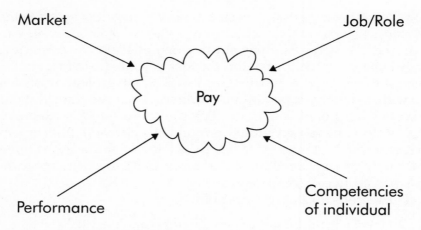

Figure 9.1 Factors Influencing Pay

● the market.

The real issue is how to achieve the best balance between these factors to meet particular business requirements and circumstances: this is explored later in this chapter.

If this balance is achieved, then relating pay to competencies can have a powerful and positive impact, by rewarding and encouraging the behaviours which the organisation needs to achieve success, in a realistic and practical context.

TERMINOLOGY

Some commonly used terminology does cause problems. The term 'competency based pay' is probably the most widely used general label for a wide range of approaches involving skills and competencies, but this terminology does lead to misunderstandings.

In the first instance, competency *based* pay may be taken to imply that pay is only based on competencies, and hence cannot also be based upon performance, on role, or on the other factors noted earlier. A much more accurate description is competency *related* pay, which does not imply this exclusivity of approach, and better describes the more balanced approach which is normally needed.

Second, the word competency in the pay context is often used loosely, covering technical skills as well as behavioural competencies. Some pay schemes described as competency based pay are in reality purely based on the acquisition of technical or practical skills, and would more accurately be described as skill based (or related) pay.

For clarity in the pay debate, it helps to distinguish clearly between those technical and practical *skills*, which are more readily amenable to training and direct accreditation and which represent a threshold for people to perform satisfactorily in a role; and the more deeply seated behavioural *competencies* which may take longer to develop, and which make the difference between adequate and high performance in a role. Pay may be related to either one or to both, but it is important to recognise which is being adopted, and why. Skill related pay is used to encourage skill development – for example to foster multi-skilling, or to reward progression through a skill-based technical ladder. On the other hand, competency related pay may be used to reinforce particular behaviours (eg customer service behaviours, team behaviours), or to reinforce those more specific behaviours which correlate with high performance in a role.

ACHIEVING THE BALANCE

To get the best balance between the various factors which may determine pay, we need to pose the basic question – what do we want to pay people *for*? Overall levels of pay will be influenced by the external market, and the organisation's required relationship to that market, given its business performance and its overall plans and strategies. But decisions about how individuals are then paid within the organisation, how they are positioned relative to each other, and how their pay is progressed require us to answer this basic question.

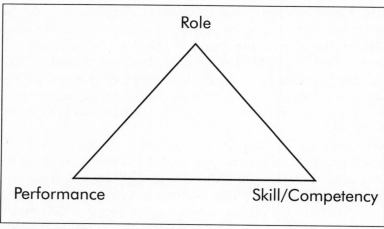

Figure 9.2 What should we pay people for?

The options are limited. In principle we can pay people for the job or role they carry out (as in the traditional model); for their capability (ie, the skills and competencies which they bring); or for the performance they achieve.

Earlier in this chapter, we described the inadequacies of basing pay purely on role or capability. Basing pay purely on performance is equally limited in its perspective. A balance needs to be struck which fits the needs of the particular business.

WORK CULTURES

A useful approach to determining the best balance is through consideration of the work culture of the organisation. The distinctive work culture of an organisation is not something that happens by chance or decree. Rather, it is driven by the nature of its business and the forces which operate on it. Hay's research on a large number of organisations identified two sets of opposing forces, which determine the work culture which exists.

- Is the business driven mainly by its own capability or technology, or by the demand of the customer?

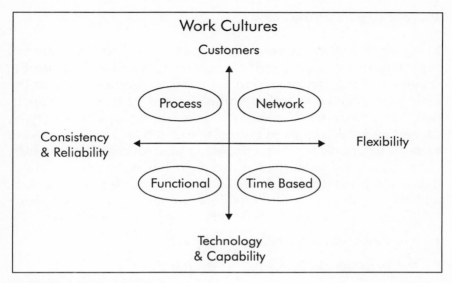

Figure 9.3 Work Cultures

- Is it driven more by the need for consistency and reliability of delivery or by the need for flexibility?

All organisations are driven to some degree by all these requirements. But the balance between these opposing forces is a major determinant of the work culture which exists.

Functional Work Culture

In a functional work culture, characterised by the need to deliver the organisation's capability, efficiently and consistently, the organisation is likely to be based on functional specialisation, with clearly defined roles in a stable, structural arrangement. This is in line with the traditional approach to organisations described at the start of this chapter. Issues of job or role are likely to dominate in the pay equation, with consideration of performance and skills and competencies in a subordinate position. This is not the most likely environment in which strongly competency-related pay is likely to work.

Process Work Culture

Many organisations have moved dramatically from an internal capability focus to an external customer focus. The most notable examples of this can be seen in the financial services sector, in the wake of deregulation and radically changed patterns of competition. The process work culture which results is characterised by an organisational emphasis on business processes, and widespread use of multi-functional teamworking rather than functional hierarchies.

In this environment, roles need to be much more flexibly defined, representing a balance between the needs of the business and the capability of the individual. Traditional job descriptions need to be replaced by more flexible role profiles, identifying

- the contribution required from the role;
- the skills needed to operate in the role;
- the competencies needed to perform in the role.

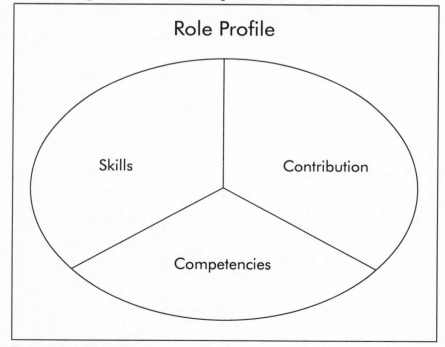

Figure 9.4 Role Profile

Within a particular area of work, it may help to define a series of role profiles describing work of different levels – ie, different levels of contribution enabled by different levels of skills and competencies. Such groupings of roles where the nature of work is similar but the level is differentiated are often referred to as job families. In the pay equation, the issues of role, of individual capability and of performance need to be much more in balance, to reflect this type of work culture.

This is usually achieved by adopting a pay structure of fewer, wider grades. This does not remove the impact of job/role size or the need for some kind of job evaluation, but it reduces the sensitivity of pay to small job size differences, so enabling more focus to be placed on consideration of individual skills, competencies and performance. One of the most widespread trends in current pay management practices is the move to fewer, wider grades.

But coarsening the grade structure does not in itself *produce* a shift in emphasis from jobs to people : it just *enables* the shift to be made. Within a wider grade, decisions still have to be made about where to position each individual's pay, and how they should move through the pay range, based upon assessment of their skills, competencies and performance, in the right balance. Effective pay management thus becomes much more dependent on the quality and robustness of the processes for managing and measuring these aspects. Overall, the more we take out *structure* from pay, the stronger these *processes* need to be.

Time-Based Work Culture

Time-based work cultures, driven by the combination of technology and flexibility, are characterised by extensive use of project work, in which people continually move between project teams and in which they make their own individual contribution.

In this environment, the issues of capability and performance probably dominate over the issues of role in the pay equation. In this work culture broadbanded pay arrangements find their most useful application. The issues about managing pay in broadbands are similar to those for wider grades, but even more so, with critical reliance on the effectiveness of performance and competency assessment processes.

Network Work Culture

In this ultimate combination of customer focus and flexibility, the organisation is a loose alliance of individuals. Pay is largely unstructured, and generally based on individual contracts reflecting market worth.

RELATING PAY TO COMPETENCIES – PRACTICAL ISSUES

There are two general ways in which pay may be related to competencies. The first is by building competencies into the performance management process, as described in the previous chapter, and then relating pay movement through a pay range to assessed performance.

This may not be thought of or labelled as competency related pay and would be more commonly classified under the heading of performance related pay, but it shows the inadequacy of pigeon-holing the techniques. It is one of the most widely applicable ways of building competencies into pay considerations, and can be used effectively in most circumstances and work cultures.

The second, and more explicit way of relating pay to competencies is through the use of the role profiling or job family approach outlined earlier. This is particularly useful in managing pay progression through the wider pay bands associated with the move to fewer grades, or broadbands. It also enables competencies to be considered alongside issues of skill and contribution, to achieve a balanced approach.

To illustrate, consider the example noted earlier of a team of people working together in a customer service activity. The job family modelling technique attempts to identify the different *levels of work* which exist within that environment, and express each level of work as a role profile, identifying the skills, competencies and contribution associated with that level. Individuals are then assessed, in terms of their own skills, competencies and contribution, to identify the level of work at which each is operating.

This can then be translated into a pay structure in one of two ways.

- Each identified level of work can be expressed as a grade and from that the individual is allocated to a grade based on their assessment against the role profiles. Using this approach, a conventional grade structure is maintained, but competency consideration is explicitly built in to the grading decision. Pay movement within the pay range for each grade can be managed using a performance assessment process against the same criteria of skill, competency and contribution, up to the point where it is appropriate to trigger movement to the next grade.

- Alternatively, the role profiles can be used to identify trigger points or zones within a broad pay band. Again, individuals are assessed against the skill, competency and contribution criteria for each zone, and moved through and between the zones according to this assessment.

In principle, these two approaches are fundamentally the same. In both cases, individuals (rather than jobs) are being assessed against defined criteria – skills, competencies and contribution – and positioned into the pay structure accordingly. The difference is largely about presentation: in the first case it is presented as a grade structure, while in the second it is presented as a pattern of pay zones within a broadbanded arrangement. The choice is often based on consideration of what is culturally acceptable within a particular organisation, and the degree to which traditional grade labels need to be maintained (eg to provide explicit recognition), or to be removed, to encourage flexibility of attitude and remove artificial status barriers.

In the last few years, job family based approaches have rapidly gathered momentum and are now widely used in a range of different businesses and sectors. They do not focus on pay in isolation but provide a powerful basis for integration of the major HR management processes on a consistent basis.

The same role profiles/level of work definitions can be used to drive:

- pay and grading decisions, as described here;
- recruitment and selection decisions;
- performance management processes;
- career development processes.

These approaches do not totally replace the need for some kind of job evaluation or role sizing process. These techniques are not in conflict, but complementary. In most organisations, a number of different job families exist. While the approach described here tackles the issues of pay progression *within* a family, decisions still have to be made about pay relativities *between* families. Job evaluation (of the role profiles, not of individual jobs), provides the means to do this, in a logical and rational way – although in this context, job evaluation is being used in a very different way, and with a much lower focus than in its traditional applications.

10

Getting the Right People for the Job

Daniel Bouchard

RECRUITMENT — REDUCING TURNOVER

Recruitment and selection are enormously costly and time consuming for most organisations – and the higher the rate of
turnover in a company, the greater the costs. Yet, few companies
focus on how to:

- improve the effectiveness of the process;
- improve the quality of the candidates selected and measure
  the impact of good selection versus bad ones.

This chapter focuses on how companies can make dramatic
improvements to their recruitment and selection processes
through a process known as focused interviewing.

FOCUSED INTERVIEWING

The focused interview is a direct by-product of the behavioural
event interview (BEI) technique which was developed by
Hay/McBer.

The BEI technique is used by Hay/McBer specially trained consultants when they have to explain the variation of performance between people working in the same job, in a given context. A sample of incumbents are interviewed and they discuss, as precisely as possible, several recent job situations where they have been active participants. The purpose is to find out what high performers do that average performers do not or what they do better or more often. The interviewer does not know what he or she is looking for, the results are used in the development of a competency model.

The purpose of the focused interview is not to understand what leads to success in a job but to assess some specific competencies of a person – and their suitability for a job. In this case, the interviewer really knows what he or she is expecting from the interviewee; so the interviewer asks for situations in which there may be opportunities for the interviewee to demonstrate the specific attitudes or behaviours.

That means that the interviewer is aware of the competency model that the interviewee is being assessed against, and has control over the type of job situations that are discussed. The interviewer will ask questions like: 'Tell me about a time when you had to deal with a difficult person,' if he wants to give the interviewee a chance to relate how she demonstrated interpersonal sensitivity or influence. The questions depending of course on the competencies in the model and will be designed for specific purposes.

A focused interview may last an hour and a half to allow a fair and relevant view of a couple of personal characteristics.

In most cases focused interviews are conducted by HR professionals, but can also be by line managers. However, all interviewers must have received specific training to make sure they can use the interview technique and understand the logic behind the competency model they are to assess people against.

PREREQUISITES

Assessment may have important consequences for a person's professional and personal life. Also, the results of an assessment process have to be accepted by the people in the company. So it is important that assessors are carefully and completely trained and that the focused interview technique is integrated in a clear and comprehensive HR process.

This is why, before implementing tools and techniques, however powerful these may be, organisations must consider all aspects of communication and implementation, ie find answers to questions like: how are we going to clarify the process for interviewees, what kind of feedback are people expecting, how does this process integrate with other aspects of HR in the company, do we have answers in terms of development of competencies?

Case Study – A Bank

At the beginning of 1994, Modern Bank was just like any other financial institution belonging to the public sector, ie most human resources processes were mainly supported by a series of administrative rules, including the staffing process of the branch manager jobs, reserved for internal candidates and based on personal status and seniority and a formal interview with an HR manager.

These rules made it a matter of luck whether or not there were superior performers in the job. At the same time the evolution of the branch manager role made the job more demanding, especially in the public relations field and in the management field.

Competency model
Hay/McBer consultants conducted an expert panel to clarify the contents of the branch manager role and to highlight the superior performance indicators in the new role of branch manager. One outcome of this was identification of a sample of 12 incumbents to interview – three average performers and nine superior performers – ie more than 10% of the total population of branch managers. The interviews were conducted by Hay/McBer and a model was designed and validated by senior management.

Focused Interviews
Hay/McBer trained six people in interviewing. The training lasted two and a half days. Then, to ensure a complete understanding of the interview techniques, each trainee conducted at least one – and in some cases two – full size BEIs, each lasting between two and a

half hours and three hours. These interviews were taped, allowing a careful and in-depth review from Hay/McBer consultants and a precise feedback to interviewers, in terms of improvement areas. Following this, Hay/McBer certified the trainees as qualified interviewers, able to move on to focused interviewing.

Hay/McBer then designed a specific interviewing technique focused on the competency model of the branch manager. This technique included the following:

- a professional presentation made by the interviewee;

- a series of job situations, with at least one management situation;

- the view the interviewee had from the job.

Two interviewers had to be present with two different and complementary roles: the first and third part of the interview would be conducted by a senior HR manager whereas the middle part – a focused interview concentrating on job situations – would be conducted by a certified BEI interviewer. During that part, it was agreed that the senior HR Manager would remain silent. The purpose of such a process was to have a high quality interview made within fair and acceptable conditions from the candidates' point of view, due to the fact that they would still be able to express their views in the presence of an HR manager.

Communicating the new selection system was done at the same time as the publication of available jobs.

The process was well accepted, beyond expectations. The main reason for that was that for the first time most candidates had the opportunity to talk about themselves and what they did – not only about what they thought. The concrete nature of the interview had been a positive experience for people. The selection process has been conducted twice a year since 1994.

The benefits for the customer are of several kinds:

- The quality of job incumbents was upgraded, which reinforced commitment among the people in branches, at a moment when cost reduction was a main concern.

- There was an increase of credibility and legitimacy of HR managers through a strict, fair and professional selection process, which allowed further successful HR tools implementations.

- This success brought a review of all current selection processes: all were improved and focused interview techniques were introduced in some of them.

Further training in BEI is scheduled as newly hired HR people are now in charge of this well accepted procedure.

Case Study – Recruiting Students For A Business School

ESCM (Ecole Supérieure de Commerce de Montpellier) is a distinguished French business school and was highly placed by a recent survey of business schools. There has been tough competition among French business schools since the early 1990s; particularly they compete on how quickly students find a job after their studies.

The quality of teaching methods and the school equipment had been constantly upgraded by ESCM. They also decided in 1994 to upgrade the recruitment of students. The first step was to define precisely the target. Hay/McBer designed a competency model, taking into account three performance criteria for superior performers among recruited students:

- they would make the best possible use of the resources of the school;

- they would find a job quickly at the end of their studies;

- they would leverage this first experience to begin a career.

Hay/McBer interviewed pupils in the school, those who had recently finished their studies and were in their first job and people at the beginning of what they described as the career they wanted. An interesting part of the project was to adapt the Hay/McBer competencies to build a model for pupils, ie those who had had only a few contacts with real professional situations. The model included eight competencies among which four were critical (for example, teamwork and co-operation was seen as important, whereas self confidence was a critical competency).

Following this, Hay/McBer designed an assessment technique within the constraints of the customer ; the main constraint came simply from the number of candidates (than up to 1,500 who had passed the written exams) within a short period (ten days) and the number of assessors (about 20).

No precise profile existed in the previously used selection process. It had consisted of a quick presentation by the candidate on a randomly chosen topic (ten minutes) followed by a conversation where candidates were asked their views on various situations. The second part was completely left to the assessors, in terms of what they were looking for or how they would handle it.

We recommended three major improvements :

- a homogeneous process;

- the use of the competency model for selection, relying on an in-depth training of assessors;

- an adaptation of the focused interview.

One trained interviewer would be accompanied by a silent observer, but both would take notes on specially designed forms. Tests which were made with first year pupils showed that many of the events discussed took only 10 to 15 minutes; so the duration of the recruitment interview was set at 30 minutes, followed by a 10 minute debate between the selectors. The selectors made candidates as comfortable as possible, to allow them to give their best without pressure.

Hay/McBer designed a set of focused questions for each competency in the model. For the first year of use, the interview technique was designed as follows :

1. After a two minute introduction candidates would be given the list of questions, from which they would choose one and tell a story about it.

2. At the end of this, say 10 to 15 minutes, the interviewer would again pass the list of questions and so on until the end of the interview, recommending the candidate to take time in choosing.

3. After 30 minutes, the candidate would be firmly interrupted and thanked for his or her co-operation.

4. The selectors then made an A, B or C rating decision, which would be weighted with the candidate's results in other fields, especially languages.

From the first year of use, this procedure gave interesting results :

*   The recruited candidates were seen as highly motivated people, with a genuine desire to be in control of their lives.

*   A survey made during the interview phase showed that candidates were pleased to have an opportunity to talk about themselves, unlike the recruitment procedures of other schools.

*   The candidates also liked talking in a relaxed way, instead of facing a hostile panel, which is the way most high schools conduct selection interviews.

For the second year of use, we refined the model and designed two sets of focused questions, the first looked only at the critical competencies. The second year technique was slightly improved :

1. The first part (a two minutes presentation) remained the same, then the candidate would be given the first set of questions, among which he or she would choose one and tell a story about it.

2. At the end of the first event (i.e. after 10 to 15 minutes), the interviewer decided whether they had had enough information on the critical competencies : if so, they would move on to the second set of questions, if not, they would ask the candidate to choose another question from the first set (as candidates did not know there were two sets they would not be affected by this decision).

3. After 30 minutes, the candidate would be firmly interrupted and thanked for his or her co-operation.

4. Candidates were rated A, B or C as before.

Results

The new system had a positive impact on the school's image among students, which brought 14% more candidates the following year. The image of the school was greatly improved too, among firms which fund the school, as they could see ESCM was more customer oriented with graduates more adapted to the market. This brought an increase in funds.

At the same time the school decided to use the focused interview technique as part of students' term time work to help them assess their strong points and weaknesses when they had to choose between several specialities. The point is not to orientate students in a directive way, but to help them measure how difficult or how easy it would be for them to go into a particular professional field, and develop relevant behaviours, competencies, skills and knowledge.

Case Study – Case Europe

Case is one of the world major companies making and selling agriculture equipment and construction equipment. At the beginning of 1995, Case Europe had completed the outline for restructuring its sales & marketing department. This was considered crucial to gain more market shares in a competitive environment.

The change it wanted to implement was to rebuild relationships between Case and its network of dealers, to make a genuine partnership, mainly in three European countries: Germany, Great Britain and France. New roles had been designed for field people who would rely on new high technology tools and a quality sales support structure. The aim was to staff the new positions, primarily with the people who were in the sales field at that time, providing they could cope with the jobs.

In the first part of the project, we designed four competency models corresponding to the four roles of the new field organisation :

- business manager;

- parts business developer;

- equipment specialist;

- service specialist.

The models were built through an expert panel process because of time constraints.

After the validation of the models by senior management, Hay/McBer recommended the use of an assessment centre for the four field jobs, within the same period of time, in the three countries.

The assessment centre had to be well accepted by people who were to go through it; so we helped design a comprehensive and dedicated HR process including an assessment centre, where candidates would be observed by Case HR people and by operational managers. As often in such cases, the exercises of the assessment centre were designed similar to the realities of the jobs so that incumbents would think it relevant and acceptable, but not too close to the jobs so that non-incumbents would have no chance of success.

This assessment centre lasted nearly one day and included :

- a focused interview, lasting one hour;

- a case study, lasting one hour and a quarter;

- a presentation exercise, lasting five minutes;

- a group activity, lasting 30 minutes;

- a role play, lasting 30 minutes.

Company observers received three days training in observing and assessing behaviours in all the different exercises used and in focused interviewing. At the beginning of the assessment day all exercises were briefly explained to the group of candidates, then more details were given to the individuals just before they went through them. The four jobs had some similarities which allowed to use a single list of questions during the focused interviews which lasted an hour and followed the usual pattern.

Then the assessment centres took place in the three countries, with the constant participation of a local Hay/McBer consultant in all sessions, as did Case Europe observers. After a few sessions – what we may see as a warm-up – all the Case Europe observers realised how the interview was central in the assessment process: at the end of the assessment day when selectors discussed the competencies of the candidates, what had been observed during the interview often helped make a final decision. Some 300 people went through this process in the three European countries.

A similar process was designed for the support structure jobs and the specially designed assessment centre included focused interview too. Some 150 people went through the second process on a European scale.

Results

Case Europe has now staffed all sales and marketing positions. The overall process was well accepted and applied to internal candidates as well as external ones. Case Europe is now considering the use of the focused interview as an assessment technique for managers who have to make development recommendations to their subordinates. There is now a project to give in-depth training on focused interviews to more than 150 managers in Europe.

Case Europe was also able to have the best possible presence and effectiveness in the market at a moment when the business cycle reversed and business restarted. Shareholders appreciated this: the value of its share was $19 in June 1994 on the NY Stock Exchange and was $50 in January 1996.

CONCLUSION

From a customer's point of view, the major strong points of focused interviewing are its flexibility and its efficiency. Focused interview based selection processes can be applied to virtually any kind of competency; it is simply a matter of designing a set of questions to structure the interview with relevant events. Trained interviewers can conduct a fair and efficient process, through which they can reliably assess specific competencies of the interviewee.

Success with this technique is a matter of preparation (what job, what model, which competencies, which questions) and a matter of having perfectly trained interviewers.

It may be seen as time consuming – training and interviewing takes time – and a company which intends to use this selection process has to be ready to train a sufficient amount of resources to conduct interviews. However, Hay/McBer has developed a high quality training process for focused interviewing used in many countries. This allows Hay/McBer to conduct demanding projects simultaneously in different countries, to answer specific questions on particular populations and to help implement new ways of managing people in organisations that seemed previously unlikely to accept any change.

11

How to use Competencies in Assessment

Heather Bell

Ever since the Roman Emperor Hadrian put his prospective centurions through a gruelling week-long selection process, employers have tried to increase the quality of their selection decisions by creating an artificial environment which mimics the essential features of the job to be done. They then ask prospective candidates to submit to a battery of experiences and, on the basis of how they do, make decisions about who is in and who is out.

Some readers may have vivid 20 year-old memories of assessment centres — although we did not call them that — for university or traditional companies, in which the principal aims seemed to be to establish the polish of your table manners, or the wit of your small talk.

The past few years have, however, seen increased questioning about the value and role of assessment centres. Some companies found that the graduates they hired following a long and intensive recruitment process, including a day-long so-called 'second interview' (actually an assessment centre), did no better on average than those whom they brought in using simpler and less costly processes.

Others found that their assessment centres were remarkably good at selecting people with a certain set of values and capabilities – although the organisation had changed direction and these were no longer the values and capabilities required for the future. Even those firms which genuinely valued the output of their centres worried about the sheer amount and cost of the input: line managers in particular questioned, with increasing vigour, the return they were getting for the long days they had to invest in the process.

Inevitably the question became: how can we get more value from our assessment centres – because if we don't, we just can't afford them any more.

Some organisations have been tempted to address this question by cutting the cost of their centres. 'Why not use fewer assessors?' 'Do the assessors really need rigorous training in observation and rating – they are all experienced managers, aren't they?' 'What about doubling the number of participants on each centre?' Others have considered disguising assessment centres as something else. 'Let's run a teambuilding event and we can quietly pick up the data we need to select those new team leaders.'

In our view, such approaches are at best ineffective and at worst unethical and damaging. Assessment centres do need to be properly staffed, with the correct numbers of competent assessors and administrators. They must be rigorously designed and run, so that they reach correct and defensible conclusions and do not discriminate unfairly against those of different race, gender, religion or age. The organisation needs to have careful processes for handling and storing assessment data. These requirements can be time-consuming and expensive, yet they are a critical foundation for effective assessment centres. Organisations which cannot meet them would be wise to consider whether they should be thinking of assessment centres at all.

If cutting down on input costs is not the answer, what can an organisation can do to get real value from assessment centres? We believe that the answer is to focus the assessment on the factors that have a proven link with business success

LINKS TO BUSINESS SUCCESS

One reason why many assessment centres failed to deliver real business benefit is that they were testing for a range of characteristics that the organisation *felt* to be necessary in the job. These might have included appearance, presentation skills and tenacity for a sales person, for example. In practice, these characteristics might be those which are necessary to do the job to a satisfactory standard – so the centre, which is based exclusively on these, is likely to select individuals who do the job to a satisfactory standard. The problem is that, in a competitive environment, satisfactory is seldom enough: a satisfactory salesforce is soon overtaken if its competitors are performing excellently.

An even more dangerous scenario is when the characteristics sought by the centre do not correlate at all with performance in the job. In this case, the people hired stand only a random chance of success. An example of this was encountered recently by one of our consultants who was asked by a client to help work out why a newly-established customer services team just was not working.

Not only were client service standards slipping, but the people within the team were demotivated, with turnover rates starting to rise. 'I just don't understand it,' fretted the client, 'this team has some of the best young people in the firm – at least we thought they were.' In the event we discovered that team members had been selected using a centre that had delivered excellent results for the client in the past – and which was designed to identify people with strong leadership skills. In the high-pressure environment of customer services, however, the capability to work as a member of a team is far more important – and was not explored at all during the centre.

The assessment centre adds real value if it can find and bring in to the job people who demonstrate the characteristics that drive truly excellent performance. What these characteristics are, however, is not merely a matter of common sense. For example, one part of Hay/McBer's recent study into the characteristics of the leaders of outstandingly successful insurance companies, involved asking chief executives to identify which competencies are most important in their roles: in the event, they selected only a small number of those characteristics which were later proven, by rigorous research, to be associated with truly excellent corporate performance. A centre which is based on the factors that are relevant to performance in the job, and which is well run and properly observed, provides real support to the organisation in meeting its business objectives.

	Cognitive test	Business case study	Group exercise	Competency-based interview
Achievement drive		✔	✔	✔
Analytical thinking	✔	✔		✔
Planning & organising		✔		✔
Team working			✔	✔

Figure 11.1 Example of part of an assessment grid

Once the competency model on which the centre is to be based is in place, the second challenge is to ensure that participants have a chance to demonstrate the extent to which they possess the competencies. This needs to be done through a range of activities which, between them, provide opportunities to demonstrate the competencies. An example of a grid, showing the desired competencies and the activities in which they will be demonstrated is in Figure 11.1.

It is important that each competency should be observable in more than one activity, so that participants have several opportunities to demonstrate their capability in that area. This also helps to ensure a rounded view of each participant, as effective rotation of assessors means that each assessor observes each participant at least once.

12

Improving Management Competence at Levi Strauss

Erin Lap and Axel Peters

Levi Strauss & Co, founded in 1850 in San Francisco, is the biggest producer of branded apparel; its brands are Levi's, Dockers, Brittania and Slaters. The firm has sold about 2.5 billion pairs of jeans. Levi Strauss employs 38,000 people, the turnover is $6.7 billion with a profit of $735 million (1995).

The company is strongly focused on a number of values, which are defined in its 'aspiration statement'. This covers not only the mission and the business vision, it also concentrates on the way things are done. Values like recognition and respect, openness and diversity are highly regarded.

Internally these values are reflected in the kind of leadership managers practice (management by values and management by objectives); they are highlighted in processes (eg 'partners in performance' which is a performance management program that includes fixed and variable pay structures for all employees and the core elements of continuous learning and development), training programmes and so-called 'aspirational weekends'.

Externally the company has established 'Terms of Engagement' which govern the value based relationship between Levi Strauss & Co and its contractors/business partners. This cites, for example, that 'we will only do business with partners whose workers are in all cases present voluntarily, not put at risk of physical harm, fairly compensated, allowed the right of free association and not exploited in any way.' 'We do realise that doing so we are paying a price,' says one of the general managers of Levi Strauss.

Recently Levi Strauss has been confronted with changing demands from two sides: market trends are shifting much more quickly and retailers are demanding a new kind of partnership. To cope with these challenges successfully the European organisation started a business process re-engineering project in 1994 – called the 'European customer service initiative'. Fully in line with the company's values, executives found that successful implementation of the BPR results depends largely on people issues. 'To stay on top of change, we must be committed to improve continuously not only what we do but how we do it,' (Carl von Buskirk, president of Levi Strauss Europe). As part of the project a competencies programme was initiated before the end of the BPR project.

PROJECT PURPOSE AND REQUIREMENTS

The target was to get an inventory of the talents in the organisation, to encourage further development, actively involving employees in the process, and to find the best match between employees and future jobs. The programme should make sure that employees could cope with changes in the redesigned organisation and fulfil its aims.

The company decided to adopt a competency based approach: to look at those behaviours that make the difference between adequate and excellent performance. Hay/McBer was chosen as external consultant to help. Due to the unfinished BPR process the organisation structure and the new roles were not clear enough to develop concise competency profiles per role. Another way had to be found. The approach developed had the following characteristics:

- the competencies had to reflect future management requirement;

- instead of developing profiles per role, one set of competencies would be developed, containing all relevant competencies for managerial jobs;

- an efficient yet reliable assessment process consisting of a 360° approach and a behavioural event interview;
- the assessment process would be introduced in all European countries involved in four months and allow participants to use their native languages.

Levi's and Hay/McBer identified 21 competencies. These were presented with clear behavioural descriptions, so managers could recognise them easily and start to apply them. The assessment process itself had to be efficient yet reliable. It was decided to assess all managers by:

- an in-depth interview by an external consultant;
- a 360° assessment, using questionnaires.

The main reasons for this were that, next to a clear and reliable picture of (potential) competencies, an important predictor of success is found in proven performance, as perceived by people we work with. The 360° approach was feasible because of Levi's culture of openness and executives are accustomed to giving feedback via an already existing 360° focusing on value based managment.

The buy-in of the managers involved was crucial, even more so to ensure the success of the 360° process. As a first step all country or general managers were informed about the assessment process: its purpose, the steps and the consequences. After this the management teams were briefed by the general manager, assisted by Hay/McBer consultants.

Each participant was asked to fill in a questionnaire him/herself to nominate colleagues and subordinates to fill in questionnaires, as well as his or her boss. All questionnaires were sent directly to Hay/McBer to be processed. Each manager was interviewed by a Hay/McBer consultant. Hay/McBer used the behavioural event interview technique. The information provided by the interviewees contains a lot of data on competencies. Afterwards, many interviewees acknowledged that they revealed more than they had intended; and the interview itself helped them to clarify certain questions.

We drew up the assessment reports, using the questionnaire results and interview data. The questionnaire data provided much information about the competencies as demonstrated in the job.

The integration of interview data and questionnaire results made it possible to identify:

- competencies an individual possessed and demonstrated;

- competencies an individual had, yet were not perceived by others;

- developmental areas for the individual.

Based on this analysis, feedback was given to the participants, presented in graphs (see Figure 12.1) and explained in a four page report. The strong and weaker points per cluster were described. We also compared the assessment results with what excellent performers do and indicated what – in our professional opinion – kept the participant from demonstrating the competency effectively. We then made recommendations on development.

Soon after the individual received the report we held a meeting with him or her to discuss it. Participants often saw themselves dif-

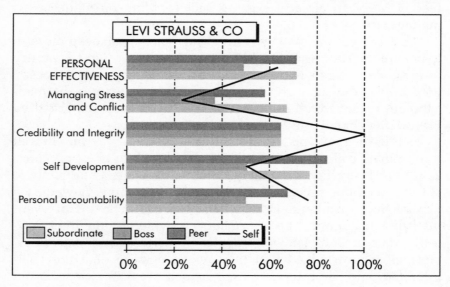

Figure 12.1 Competency rating

ferently from the way their superiors, colleagues and subordinates perceived them. This is inevitable as people behave differently with different people in order to be successful. For some participants however there were unpleasant surprises. It is not flattering to accept that your subordinates do not see you as having management skills. In the feedback meetings, the consultant helped the participant to interpret the data and to decide on developmental objectives and plans, although it was always up to the participant and his or her superior to draw up his or her own plan.

It was agreed beforehand that all participants, if they agreed with the assessment results, would discuss these and their own conclusions with their superior. These meetings were held shortly after the feedback meeting with the consultant. In these meetings the participant had the opportunity to talk about learning points, the developmental objectives and the support he or she needed. The developmental objectives were made a part of the performance management cycle, and considered as appraisal criteria. By doing so the assessment results were integrated in the managerial practices.

Next, all assessment reports were sent to the European headquarters. This enabled Levi's to set up a database, containing reliable information on the managers' actual and potential talents. Based on experiences of the assessment process, the 360° questionnaire was adjusted so that it could be used for assessment of the next management level.

The next major steps for Levi's are to:

- assess the direct reports of MT-members;

- develop the process for the managers assessed;

- move to competency based selection of managers.

In the future months an analysis of all 360° data will be conducted to check its validity and possible cultural differences.

ADDED VALUE

The management of Levi's is convinced that they have made a major step forward. Although before this project they were accustomed to performance management practices, and worked with criteria derived from their values, they now acknowledged that the competencies approach added additional value to the overall development objectives.

The process provided them with a 'language' to talk on personal characteristics in a new and focused way. The behavioural descriptors of competencies and the need to argue with real life examples improved communication even in the very communicative Levi's environment.

The assessed participants got a complete 360° picture of the competencies in a common standard – a unique experience. The developmental plans derived and the ongoing communication on the behaviours that make the difference between average and superior performance will help Levi's to meet the challenges of the future.

Index